BRUCE WEBER'S
★ INSIDE ★
PRO FOOTBALL
◇ 1987 ◇

SCHOLASTIC INC.

New York Toronto London Auckland Sydney

Scholastic Books are available at special discounts for quantity purchases for use as premiums, promotional items, retail sales through specialty market outlets, etc. For details contact: Special Sales Manager, Scholastic Inc., 730 Broadway, New York, NY 10003.

ISBN 0-590-40799-6

Copyright © 1987 by Scholastic Books, Inc.
All rights reserved. Published by Scholastic Inc.

12 11 10 9 8 7 6 5 4 3 2 1   7 8 9/8 0 1/9

Printed in the U.S.A.   01

First Scholastic printing, September 1987

CONTENTS

INTRODUCTION:
The Road to San Diego

About 103,000 fans and assorted others managed to see Super Bowl XXI in more or less comfortable seats at the Rose Bowl last January. Another 10,000 or so never made it. They were members of a famous sports group: the "if I'm there, I'll manage to get in" association. Last year they didn't. For money you can buy just about anything. Except at Super Bowl XXI, that is. It was an amazing sight to watch.

If those folks thought last year was bad, wait until *this* year. Super Bowl XXII is scheduled for the last day in January of 1988. The site is San Diego's Jack Murphy Stadium. There are just about 60,000 seats, about 40% fewer than the Rose Bowl. About the only sure way to guarantee yourself a seat is to play for one of the competing teams. And that's what the 28 NFL teams will be working for, beginning September 13.

Even that isn't certain. Labor problems — players vs. owners — were the major topics of conversation during the off-season. Both groups well remembered 1982, when a strike reduced the season from 16 games to nine. The memory is anything but pleasant.

Assuming cooler heads prevail (and the season moves without a break from September 13 through December 28), there may well be some changes at the top of the league standings.

Although our New Jersey neighbors will holler, we believe the Giants will find repeating as difficult as "they" say it is. Basically the Giants were lucky to win last year. No, not lucky to win their games — they were awesome. Lucky to stay healthy. While rivals were falling all over the place, the Giants kept sending out the same fellows every week. If the Giants are lucky again, they can do it again.

Meanwhile the NFC races will be brutal. If Dexter Manley is sound and Jay Schroeder continues to improve, the Washington Redskins could well sit atop the NFC East. If the Chicago Bears finally find an effective quarterback who can play, let's say, 14 of the 16 games on the schedule, the Bears could well return to the Super Bowl. If Joe Montana stays healthy and the 49ers forget their 49–3 blow-out to the Giants last January, they could be right in there. But our choice is the team from Disneyland — the L.A. Rams. The big "if" here is quarterback Jim Everett. If he's the real thing, then the Rams will fly. They've got a great running game and a superb defense. (Having the Rams, who play just two hours by auto from San Diego, in the Super Bowl will not help the ticket grabbers a bit!)

Our choice in the AFC: the Cleveland Browns. For trivia buffs, know that the L.A. Rams were, until 1945, the Cleveland Rams.

When they bolted for Hollywood, the Cleveland Browns (organized and coached by Paul Brown) took over the town, as part of the All-American Football Conference. Those Browns dominated the new league, then went on to become an NFL power when the AAFC went out of business after the 1949 season. The Browns-Rams rivalry was tough then and could heat up again this January.

We like the Seattle Seahawks in the AFC West (no "indoor" team has ever played in the Super Bowl) and the Miami Dolphins (with a shored-up defense) in the AFC East.

The 1987 schedule, assuming it comes off as scheduled, looks super. On the first Monday night telecast, the last two Super Bowl champions, the Giants and Bears, lock up at Chicago's Soldier Field. Could this be the start of something big?

Meanwhile, if anyone has two extra tickets to Super Bowl XXII, please call my office. Enjoy!

— Bruce Weber

National Football League All-Pro Team

Wide Receiver
AL TOON
NEW YORK JETS

The Jets' Al Toon has one of those great sports names. When you hear the chant "T-o-o-o-o-o-n" following another spectacular catch, you can't tell whether they're cheering or b-o-o-o-ing. Hint: In the Jersey Meadowlands, they're always cheering.

That's because in two years, the one-time Wisconsin U. star has shown Jets' fans that he's on his way to becoming one of the game's best — maybe ever. He owns great hands, great speed, and great leaping ability. Those are all the ingredients of a *little* wide receiver. The difference is that Toon (6–4, 200 pounds) certainly isn't little. He's the kind of athlete coaches dream about when they design their "perfect wide receiver" on paper.

A catch between his legs against Seattle in '86 proved that no ball is uncatchable when the not-too-serious Toon is around. (It was one of 85 catches for 1,176 yards and 8 TDs.) While everyone in New York and New Jersey cheered (and the fans in Seattle's Kingdome did not yell T-o-o-o-on), the Jets' young star laughed all the way to the bench.

Though the Jets have problems on defense and their running game is spotty, the pass attack, led by Toon, is first-rate.

Wide Receiver
JERRY RICE
SAN FRANCISCO 49ERS

We had a ton of trouble picking our No. 2 All-Pro wide receiver. There was no question, however, about No. 1. He's Jerry Rice, the 49ers' Mr. Excitement. His great ability alone should keep QB Joe Montana at the top of his game for many years to come.

Niner fans still can't believe the unforced fumble that killed an opening drive in the play-offs last season. But the Niners lost that one 49–3, and they would never have been there at all without the 6–2, 200-pounder from tiny Mississippi Valley State.

After only two seasons, the sure-handed, lightning-quick Rice promises to be one of the NFL's all-timers. Last season he grabbed 86 passes, tops among NFL wideouts, for 1,570 yards. That's an average of 18.3 per catch. He also scored 15 TDs on receptions, three more than any other NFL receiver. Last year, as the Niners struggled through their two seasons (with and without Montana), Rice became the major focus of opponent defenses.

Jerry's ability to go deep opens up the entire midrange area (15 to 25 yards). He gets so much respect from defenders that he can drive them deep and come back for the ball.

3

Tight End
MARK BAVARO
NEW YORK GIANTS

It was the play that made the Giants' December, maybe even their season. Trailing the 49ers 17–0 on a Monday night in California, New York's Phil Simms launched a quick pass over the middle to his big tight end Mark Bavaro. A short gain for a first down — to everyone except Bavaro, the 6–4, 245-pounder from Notre Dame. Hit first by LB Michael Walter at the 38, Bavaro kept moving. Three more Niners jumped aboard, but even three quarters of a ton of Bill Walsh's finest talent couldn't bring Bavaro down. The players all tumbled to the turf at the 18, for a 30-yard gain that got the Giants going. They rallied to win 21–17 and, going into the '87 season, still haven't lost.

After only two years, Bavaro is becoming the standard by which tight ends are measured. He is the finest blocking TE in the league, catches the ball in traffic in close, and has shown a fine ability to get deep when that's needed.

Success hasn't changed the one-time Danvers, MA, high school star. He's honest, friendly, and extremely quiet. The Giants could save money by paying him by the word. Whatever they pay, however, Bavaro's a bargain.

Tackle
JIM
COVERT
CHICAGO BEARS

They call Penn State, Linebacker U. That's because the Nittany Lions have produced so many great NFL linebackers. If that's the case, then arch-rival Pitt must be Offensive Lineman U. The Panthers' alumni group includes a couple of current All-Pros (Jim Covert of the Bears and Bill Fralic of the Falcons), a near All-Pro (Russ Grimm of the Redskins), and a flood of others.

Chicago's Covert may be the best of the bunch. The 6-4, 275-pounder is the year-in, year-out star offensive tackle in the NFL. Last year was typical. Despite playing hurt most of the time, Covert was the leader of a Bear line that again helped to produce the NFL's top rushing attack. Credit Walter Payton and Matt Suhey and friends, of course. But Covert and his mates made most of it happen.

One of the top drive blockers in football, Covert also helped the Bears cut their sack total in half in '86, even though the quarterbacks were named Flutie, Fuller, and Tomczak instead of McMahon most of the time. Michigan's Jim Harbaugh, the top Bear draft pick, adds another candidate at quarterback.

Payton is surely headed for the Hall of Fame; Covert will lead the way.

5

Tackle
ANTHONY MUNOZ
CINCINNATI BENGALS

Take a look at Anthony Munoz. Remember that he played his college ball a couple of miles from Hollywood, at Southern Cal. If you didn't know better, you'd swear that Munoz was built in a special-effects shop next to a sound stage.

The man is positively huge at 6–6 and 278 pounds. He takes up an awful lot of space on the Cincinnati Bengals' offensive line. The word around the NFL is that Munoz is the best blocker in the league. We won't argue. (Did you ever *really* see this guy?)

When Anthony came out of USC, there was no question about his ability, just his knees. And they have spent some time on the operating table (medical, not special effects). Still he hasn't missed a game in seven years, a record that merits congratulations in the NFL.

Despite the knees, the great size, and years of NFL action in the pits, Munoz remains one of the quicker tackles in the league. He's blessed with great agility and more than adequate speed. Having played in six straight Pro Bowls, Munoz plans for many more of the same.

Says Bengal coach Sam Wyche, "Anthony is surely one of the finest players in the NFL."

Guard
BILL
FRALIC
ATLANTA FALCONS

When we picked the Falcons' huge guard Bill Fralic for this post a year ago, we got plenty of questions concerning our mental balance. "How could you pick a second-year guy on an All-Pro offensive line?" the critics wanted to know.

Thanks to Fralic's performance, however, all we have to do now is rest our case. The Falcons' outstanding running game relies heavily on the super run-blocking provided by the one-time Pitt strongboy. He's not bad on pass protection, but there is practically no one in his class on the run.

New Falcon coach Marion Campbell will also benefit from Fralic's all-around ability. When injuries wiped out the Atlanta tackles again last year, Fralic moved over and never missed a beat.

Having Fralic on the offensive line is like having an 18-wheeler on board. He cuts a wide, flat path in the defense when he fires out and drives his man back down field. Blessed with great size and excellent strength, Fralic should be leading Atlanta runners for years to come.

"We look to Bill to lead our offensive line," says Marion Campbell. "It's a hard-working group with talent. With Bill in there, they'll get it done."

7

Guard
DENNIS HARRAH
LOS ANGELES RAMS

The Rams' quarterback often needs to be introduced — to Ram fans and teammates alike. L.A. is always searching for the QB who will lead them to the Super Bowl. (Young Jim Everett is the latest "hope" of the Anaheim team.)

But, to put it in political terms, there's one Ram who needs no introduction. He's Dennis Harrah, and he has been protecting those throwers since 1975. He continues to do the best job in the West now and, seemingly, forever.

At age 33, forever may well be right around the corner for the former Miami, FL, star. Meanwhile he remains one of the best run-blockers around. Eric Dickerson is eternally grateful.

There are players who are quicker than the 6-5, 250-pound Harrah. And there are a whole bunch with far more athletic ability. But Dennis is a wise old pro who knows what he's doing out there. It's called game savvy, and it comes with a decade or more of experience. He's tremendously dedicated to getting his man, which is basically what his position is all about.

If the passing game ever matches up to the Rams' running attack, L.A. could be headed to San Diego in January.

Center
DWIGHT STEPHENSON
MIAMI DOLPHINS

Baseball managers like to build a team with strength up the middle. Dolphin head coach Don Shula would agree. Miami's super offense is built on the same principle. It's no accident that Dan Marino is the All-Pro quarterback. He has football's best center, Dwight Stephenson, playing in front of him.

Though Stephenson isn't the biggest center in the game, he more than makes up for it with great strength and quickness. The 6–2, 255-pounder from Alabama has been the game's No. 1 center for the last five years. And he has done it at one of the toughest positions on the field. Defenses are geared to fouling up the center, often putting a noseman right in his face, ready to attack while the center is completing the snap.

But Stephenson can handle it. Although he has plenty of help on the Miami offensive line, particularly from guard Roy Foster, he's the main reason why Miami has allowed the fewest QB sacks over the last four seasons.

According to Shula, Dwight's work habits are among the best he's ever seen. Not a bad endorsement from someone who should know.

9

Quarterback
DAN MARINO
MIAMI DOLPHINS

A porous defense finally caught up with the Dolphins, who sank quickly in the AFC East. But Miami's problems only served to prove the greatness of its quarterback, Dan Marino.

The rangy Marino, who has been our All-Pro choice for years, gets the job done no matter what the circumstance. Even when his team is losing by basketball scores, he stands in there, gets the ball off quickly, and watches his receivers do the rest. Coach Don Shula took drastic measures to shore up the Dolphin defense during the past off-season (including a re-do of the coaching staff). But the offense seems in great hands for years to come.

Though pushed by Dave Kreig of Seattle and Ken O'Brien of the Jets (most of the season), Marino still wound up as the AFC's top-rated QB (60.5% completions, a whopping 44 TDs, and 4,746 passing yards). He became only the third QB in NFL history to throw for 4,000-plus yards for three consecutive seasons. No one as young as the 26-year-old Marino has ever done it.

Fans of Kreig, O'Brien, the Vikings' highly rated Tommy Kramer, and the Giants' heroic Phil Simms may argue. But Dan's our man.

Running Back
JOE MORRIS
NEW YORK GIANTS

Early in Joe Morris's career with the Giants, neither he nor the team was doing much. In his rare playing appearances, he heard plenty from the boo-birds. Whenever he'd goof, and that was fairly often, they'd holler, "Get the midget out of there!"

Joe is no bigger today. But the little guy from Syracuse, who seems to be able to cut on a dime, is the fans' favorite.

Why not? His team is on top — and threatening to stay there, and he is providing a rushing attack the likes of which New York (and New Jersey) hasn't seen in decades.

Morris, who shoved such immortals as Jim Brown, Floyd Little, and Larry Csonka out of the Syracuse record book, is rapidly doing the same in the pros. After sitting on the bench for most of three seasons, Morris became a Giant starter in mid-1984 and now has enjoyed 2½ amazing seasons in the driver's seat. The compact 5–7, 205-pounder has rushed for 2,852 yards the last two years, along with 35 TDs. He owns a unique ability to cut at full speed, which makes bigger opponents overrun him; and his size allows him to hide behind his offensive line, which makes him hard to find.

11

Running Back
ERIC DICKERSON
LOS ANGELES RAMS

Around Anaheim, CA, the Rams' home, the word is, "As Eric Dickerson goes, so goes L.A." It's not quite true, of course. The Rams' defense is first-rate, and there are high hopes for young QB Jim Everett. But Dickerson has been the L.A. offense for years, with no sign of slippage showing.

On the field, Dickerson looks like something out of *Star Wars*. Big (6–3, 218 pounds) and strong, he ambles around the field with his mouthpiece firmly tucked in and his goggles in place. Many Ram opponents also believe that Dickerson is out of this world, too. The one-time SMU superstar bounced back from an "off" year (for him, not normal backs) in '85. After setting an all-time record with 2,105 rushing yards in '84, Dickerson fell to 1,200 yards (and missing two games) in '85. But '86 was vintage Dickerson, with 1,821 yards on 404 carries (a 4.5-yards-per-carry average) last year. And although the Giants' Joe Morris (14), the 'Skins' George Rogers (18), and the Cowboys' Herschel Walker (12) scored more rushing TDs, none was more valuable to his team than Eric.

Dickerson's work capacity impresses coach John Robinson. "He was better than ever in '86," says the head Ram.

Defensive End
RULON
JONES
DENVER BRONCOS

When you talk about big-play people in football, you usually think about speedy wide receivers, breakaway running backs, or power-throwing quarterbacks. You hardly ever think about a defensive end.

Rulon Jones, however, is just that guy for the AFC-champion Broncos. His safety in Denver's 22–17 play-off victory over the Patriots was a key play on the Orange Crush's road to Pasadena. A one-time second-round draft pick from Utah State, Jones has become a key member of the Broncs' sack attack ever since teaming up with Karl Mecklenburg a couple of seasons back. Jones, a 6–6, 260-pounder, had 10 sacks in '85, then 13½ last year, on the way to becoming a Pro Bowl regular.

Jones's safety on Patriot QB Tony Eason was his second of the season and fourth of his career. It won the Broncos' first postseason victory since '78. But is Jones a safety specialist? The record seems to show it.

"He's an excellent pass-rusher to begin with," says his boss, Denver defensive head man Joe Collier. "Then he seems to have a nose for the football when the other team is backed up deep. The New England situation was perfect. They were behind late and had to throw. Then Rulon just let it go!"

Defensive End
DEXTER MANLEY
WASHINGTON REDSKINS

A year ago we discussed Lawrence Taylor's challenge in coming back from an off-field problem. He came all the way back. This year's candidate is the Redskins' super-tough defensive end Dexter Manley. If Dexter can put his problems behind him (and we think he can), and if he can solve the challenge of the New York Giants' Brad Benson, he'll return to the top of the All-Pro defensive-end list.

Though the Giants certainly seemed to have Manley's number, he excelled against everyone else. His total of 18½ sacks was tops among the league's down linemen, and he was a key in bringing the 'Skins to the NFC championship game (where Benson & Co. shut him down).

Manley was always among the top pass-rushers. Opponents' passing games are geared to stopping the fierce charge of the 6–3, 240-pounder from Oklahoma. But he was always suspect against the run. Manley's hard work has paid off. Now he's just about as good either way, which makes him our All-Pro choice.

Off the field, Manley talks plenty. He makes great newspaper copy. It's good for the 'Skins that he backs up his words on the field.

STEVE McMICHAEL
CHICAGO BEARS

Here's a nervous vote for the big gun in the middle of the Bears' defense, Steve McMichael. Why nervous? Because the Eagles' USFL refugee Reggie White is making rapid strides toward the top. And Kansas City's Bill Maas is quick, mean, and hungry, and itching to become the top guy.

Still we'll stick with McMichael, who is a prime mover in the Bears' defense, which gives more credit to linebackers and safeties then it does to linemen.

Few defensive tackles are better in getting to the passer than the 6–2, 265-pounder from Texas. He had eight sacks in '86, playing a position that limits a player's ability to run up an impressive sack total. But that's not McMichael's biggest asset. He's super at jamming up the run, which is what made the Bears' defense so tough last season. Giant fans think that their man Jim Burt is the best run-stopper. But all things considered, McMichael does more things better.

Defensively the Bears are as good as anyone in the game. If the offense catches up to McMichael & Co., these Bears won't hibernate until after Supe XXII next January in San Diego.

15

Outside Linebacker
LAWRENCE TAYLOR
NEW YORK GIANTS

A year ago, Lawrence Taylor's future was in doubt. (Not by us, however. We predicted he'd be better than ever.) Once the most feared defender in the NFL, LT had slipped badly, then admitted that he had off-field problems. Would he bounce back?

Taylor answered the question on the field last year. Combining the speed of a running back with the strength of a tackle, Taylor was, once again, a fearsome force. Giant opponents couldn't run away from him, couldn't block him, and couldn't stop his teammates, either. Defensive power made the Giants the NFL's best, and Taylor was the unquestioned leader.

No one in the league had more sacks than the former U. of North Carolina powerhouse. The 6–3, 243-pound Taylor racked up 20½ sacks, including six on Redskin QB Jay Schroeder during two regular-season meetings. Giant rivals stayed late at planning sessions, figuring ways to halt the Taylor Express. They tried three-man patterns, two-man patterns, and more. None of them worked.

There's no longer any question about LT's ability or desire. The only question is his rank on the all-time list of outside 'backers. No. 1 may not be far off the mark.

KARL MECKLENBURG

DENVER BRONCOS

If they made Karl Mecklenburg's story into a TV movie, they'd have to call it *Now You See Him, Now You Don't!* or *The Case of the Portable Defender!* A one-time college walk-on (a nonscholarship player at the U. of Minnesota) and rock-bottom draft choice (Denver's 12th-round pick in 1983), Mecklenburg made the Bronco team as a special-teams man and has now become an every-year All-Pro, playing seven different spots for Denver.

The 6–3, 250-pounder lines up at middle LB in the Broncos' 4–3 alignment. Then he shifts — almost anywhere. Bronco opponents are likely to find Karl at left end, nose tackle, right end, or any inside or outside linebacker spot.

"I really enjoy playing inside linebacker," says Karl. "I think I'm best suited to play there. I also enjoy playing defensive end. It's great to rush the passer up front. I hate playing nose tackle. You're always getting double-teamed. It's the toughest position in the game in my opinion."

The 27-year-old Mecklenburg was second among the Broncos in sacks (9½) and tackles (127) a year ago. His level of play, however, was All-Pro by every standard.

17

Inside Linebacker
MIKE SINGLETARY
CHICAGO BEARS

Mike Singletary of the Chicago Bears is either (choose one) the worst enemy or the best friend of the football helmet industry. In his 10 years of college (Baylor) and pro football, the Bears' monster LB has destroyed a dozen and a half of the nation's best headgear. It means either that helmets aren't what they used to be or that Singletary is one of the most punishing tacklers in the game.

We believe that today's helmets are better than ever, which leads to the conclusion that Singletary is something else. As inside linebackers go (Mike plays in the middle of the Bears' 4–3 setup), Singletary is a little short (6–0) and a little light (around 230). But he's built like a small truck, and though he's mild-mannered off the field, he's a tiger (well, a bear) when the ball is teed up.

Early in his Chicago career, Singletary was used only in "obvious run" situations. Buddy Ryan, then the defensive boss, didn't think much of Mike's work against the pass. So the one-time second draft pick worked and worked on his pass defense techniques. It didn't take long for Singletary to master the antipass game. Now he's one of the best — by any standard.

Outside Linebacker
WILBER MARSHALL
CHICAGO BEARS

Though his opposite number, Giant Lawrence Taylor, is now considered the most destructive force in football, the Bears' Wilber Marshall is possibly just as dangerous.

Their styles differ greatly. Taylor prefers to get into the opponents' backfield to disrupt the action; Marshall prefers to roam around the field, sticking his nose (and face mask, of course) into the opponents' business. Taylor's greatest assets are his strength and size. Wilber makes his living on super speed and tremendous quickness. You can't run at him, over him, or around him. And you never know when he'll be in the area against the pass. This guy does it all.

It's hard to tell what might have happened to Marshall had Al Harris not held out on the Bears during the '85 season. But when Harris sat out, Marshall stepped in — to the delight of everyone in Chicago. He's the big-play man on Chicago's big-play defense.

The Bear stoppers are loaded with talent, including Steve McMichael, Mike Singletary, and Dave Duerson; but Marshall is usually the main man when the chips are down.

19

Cornerback
LEROY IRVIN
LOS ANGELES RAMS

When you hear about the Rams' Dark Side, don't start thinking about Darth Vader or Luke Skywalker. Instead, think about the team's defensive right side, which is ably manned by Mike Wilcher, Reggie Doss, and outstanding cornerback LeRoy Irvin.

Now in his eighth year, the man from Kansas has become a fixture in the Rams' — and the NFC's Pro Bowl—defensive backfield. There's plenty of competition for All-Pro starting assignments in the NFC, including Irvin's teammate Jerry Gray and Washington's bolt of lightning, Darrell Green. But the one-time third-round draft choice has his game all together, which is good enough for us.

Ask the Patriots' head coach, Ray Berry. He watched (helplessly) as Irvin picked off two errant Pat passes last year (though New England rallied to win). In all, LeRoy picked off six passes, returning one for a touchdown, a 50-yarder, originally launched by Dallas's Steve Pelleur. That's typical for Irvin. Last year he averaged 25 yards every time he picked off an aerial.

If the Rams ever find a passing game to go with Eric Dickerson's running and their solid defense, they'll be tough to beat in the NFC West.

HANFORD DIXON

CLEVELAND BROWNS

Quiet please, everyone. This meeting of the Hanford Dixon Fan Club will come to order. Who would like to speak first? Okay, Cleveland coach Marty Schottenheimer:

"We were looking at the films late last season. Over the first 13 games, only nine or 10 passes were caught on Hanford. That's great."

Thank you, Coach. I suppose you're pretty pleased with Hanford. His seventh season this year should be even better. Now who else would like to speak? How about you, Cris Collinsworth of the Bengals?

"All I can say is that I vote for Hanford for the Pro Bowl every year. I'm glad he was finally selected last season. I came into the league with Hanford, and he has gotten better every year."

Great, Cris. Dan Fouts, you're next.

"I think that Hanford and Frank Minnifield are the best cornerbacks in the AFC. They may not get as much publicity as some others. But our team, the Chargers, have known about them for quite a while."

Now, as president of the fan club, I can tell you that we love the 5–11, 186-pounder who was our top draft pick in 1981. It's hard to believe that he had five intercepts last year. No one threw in his area. He's terrific.

Safety
DAVE DUERSON
CHICAGO BEARS

It took a contract holdout by former Pro Bowl safety Todd Bell to win a starting position in the Bears' secondary for Dave Duerson. Given that shot, the ex-Notre Damer has made the most of it. He has now played in two straight Pro Bowls himself, and Bell, though back, can just look on.

The 6–1, 208-pounder is a fierce hitter. More than one NFL quarterback has picked himself up off the ground and asked for the license number of the truck that hit him. The number is 22, and it's worn by Duerson, whose safety blitzes have made him the terror of the Chicago secondary. Dave's seven sacks last year were the most by a Bear defensive back in two decades.

Perhaps the rivalry with ex-Bear defense boss Buddy Ryan was the cause, because Duerson had his best game last year vs. his old coach's new team, the Philadelphia Eagles. All Dave managed to do was make 12 tackles, one sack, one interception — and he forced a fumble in OT that set up the winning score. Not a bad day's work.

Duerson is just a solid citizen on defense. His 109 tackles gave him third place among all of the Bears, and his six interceptions were second only to left corner Mike Richardson (with seven).

Safety
DERON CHERRY
KANSAS CITY CHIEFS

When Deron Cherry finally hangs up his helmet and cleats, he may have a great future as a pickpocket. That's what NFL passers say. Cherry, who is starting his seventh season with the Kansas City Chiefs, is one of the NFL's top ball thieves, grabbing nine enemy tosses in '86, after ringing up seven in each of the three previous seasons.

Cherry's nine INTs were good for the ball-hawk title in the AFC, only one off the NFL pace set by San Francisco's Ronnie Lott. Looking for his fifth straight trip to the Pro Bowl in '87, Cherry brings more to the game than a pair of sticky fingers. He also blocked four kicks a year ago and scored two TDs. And with his 108 tackles, he racked up his fourth straight year of 100-or-more stops.

As free safeties go, Cherry has all the tools. He's both fast and strong, the perfect combination according to the charts these days.

Thievery, however, remains the key to Cherry's game. The 5–11, 190-pounder from Rutgers is everywhere for the Chiefs. His 30 steals in the last four years make him No. 1 in the league over that period. Deron aims to keep it that way.

No "indoor" team has ever made it to the
Super Bowl, but RB Curt Warner hopes to
take the Seattle Seahawks there this year.

American
Football
Conference
Team Previews

AFC East
MIAMI DOLPHINS
1986 Finish: Third
1987 Prediction: First

John Offerdahl **Lorenzo Hampton**

"Dee-fense! Dee-fense!" No, that's not the cry of the Miami Dolphins' fans. It's the cry of Miami Dolphin coach Don Shula. Offensively the Dolphins have all the tools to make the 1987 play-offs, and perhaps make a real run at Super Bowl XXII. Defensively they'll be lucky to top last year's horrible 8–8 finish.

Shula made wholesale changes in his defensive coaching staff. Tom Olivadotti, late of the Cleveland Browns and the U. of Miami, is to run "most" of the defense. The task will be awesome; the Dolphs were 26th (tied) in the league on defense a year ago.

Maybe new Dolphin Stadium, a 73,000-seat, $100-million palace will inspire the defenders. RILB John Offerdahl, who became the first Dolphin LB ever to start, as a rookie, in the Pro Bowl last season, is the kind of player defenses are built around. He had 135 tackles — 50 more than any other Dolphin. There will be changes all over the defensive unit, which saw Bob Brudzinski, Mark Brown, and Larry Kolic finish the season at LB with Offerdahl. Shula will be looking for an impact player up front, spelling T.J. Turner, Bob Baumhower, or George Little. The return of OLB Hugh Green will help.

In the secondary, Mike Smith and Paul Lankford return from injured reserve to join CBs Reyna Thompson and William Judson and safeties Bud Brown and Glenn Blackwood. The backups are Mike Kozlowski, Donovan Rose, and Donald Brown.

The offense is still one dimensional. It is spelled M-A-R-I-N-O. The running game remains puny. Lorenzo Hampton scored *all* of the Dolphins' rushing TDs a year ago, and that number was only nine. Woody Bennett, Tony Nathan, and Ron Davenport try — but it's not enough.

Fortunately Marino is the best QB in the world, and his receivers are right up there, too. Mark Duper set a club record (and joined only eight others in league history) with eight 100-yard-plus receiving games. Mark Clayton, TE Bruce Hardy, and the rest of the group are excellent. So is the offensive front line, led by All-Pro C Dwight Stephenson, All-AFC LG Roy Foster, tackles John Giesler and Greg Koch, and guards Ronnie and Larry Lee.

AFC East
NEW ENGLAND PATRIOTS
1986 Finish: First
1987 Prediction: Second

Stanley Morgan   **Ray Clayborn**

Without a roster of superstars, the Patriots continue to surprise everyone by remaining the AFC East leaders. In '86 they did it with a running game that scared absolutely no one. If Craig James can return to his 1985 form, there's no telling how far the Pats can go in '87.

A return to form of the offensive line would help, too. The addition of ex-Buc Sean Farrell (he cost three draft picks) should help. LG Paul Fairchild, who played hurt through much of last season, reminds few of ex-All-Pro John Hannah. But C Pete Brock is a solid citizen, and RG Ron Wooten should return. Ex-Pro Bowler LT Brian Holloway should bounce back from injuries in '86; and Steve Moore, Darryl Haley, and Trevor Matich should see action.

Tony Eason, who gets fewer headlines than any other top NFL quarterback, is first-rate, off a 3,328-yard season (and 61.6% completions) with 19 TDs. Eason threw 179 passes a year ago without an interception. He and backup Steve Grogan get plenty of help from an outstanding group of receivers, led by all-star Stanley Morgan, the Pats' team MVP. Irving Fryar and Stephen Starring are outstanding, too.

For the Pats to remain at the top of the AFC East, Craig James will have to gain more than 427 yards. New England fell from sixth to 28th in rushing, with little help from Tony Collins (who underwent drug rehab), Mosi Tatupu, and Robert Weathers.

The return of a healthy Kenneth Sims will bolster the New England defensive line, where rookie Brent Williams filled in for Sims a year ago. Toby Williams should be back at NT, with Garin Veris, off a fine '86, at DRE. Ex-Boston College star Mike Ruth should help if he's healthy.

Super OLB Andre Tippett should return to form if he's recovered from a 1986 knee injury. So should Clayton Weishuhn. Lawrence McGrew is a versatile performer, and Ed Williams and Brian Ingram should be ready to go. Johnny Rembert will see lots of action.

The secondary is fine, with Ray Clayborn and Ronnie Lippett at the corners, and Roland James and Fred Marion at the safeties. Lippett had eight intercepts a year ago. James is a solid tackler.

AFC East
NEW YORK JETS
1986 Finish: Second
1987 Prediction: Third

Ken O'Brien   **Dan Alexander**

Jet fans can reflect on the glory that was the team's 10–1 start in 1986. The Jets, the "other" New York team, were the best in the NFL. A "Meadowlands" Super Bowl loomed as a real possibility. Then injuries struck, the Jets did not win another regular-season game, and the memory of the 10–1 start may have to keep the faithful going.

Funny thing about it. Though the defense was struck down by the injuries, the offense disappeared, too. QB Ken O'Brien, rolling along with the best in the league, slipped so badly that he was benched for Pat Ryan. Will O'Brien put those memories behind him in '87? RB Freeman McNeil, one of the smoothest in the league, is too often hurt. RB Johnny Hector may not be good enough. Top draftee Roger Vick will help.

The receivers, led by swift Wes Walker and coming All-Pro Al Toon on the outside and TE Mickey Shuler inside, are first-class. There's decent depth, too (JoJo Townsell, Kurt Sohn, Rocky Klever). The return of RT Reggie McElroy (knee) will help bolster the offensive line, whose main man, C Joe Fields, is 34. RG Dan Alexander is a potential star, but the others — LT Jim Sweeney, LG Ted Banker, and the rest — must improve.

The defense, of course, may be in shambles. Barring medical miracles, All-Pro NT Joe Klecko and LB Lance Mehl will not be back until midseason, if ever. DT Marty Lyons and DE Mark Gastineau will also be battling back from injuries. Youngsters like DLE Ben Rudolph, NT Tom Baldwin, and DRE Barry Bennett have possibilities. (The Jets' near-win — never should have lost — in Cleveland during the play-offs proves that.) LBs Kyle Clifton and Rusty Guilbeau and comeback star Bob Crable can do the job. The secondary, with cornerbacks Jerry Holmes and Russell Carter and safeties Leonard Lyles, Johnny Lynn, and Harry Hamilton, needs plenty of support.

The kicking game, too, is uncertain. Punter Dave Jennings seems to be kicking on borrowed time.

If the Jets get healthy — and that's an awfully *big* if — they have the ingredients to get into the swing of things in the AFC East. But Jet fans would do well to hang onto the memories of the heady start of '86.

31

AFC East
BUFFALO BILLS
1986 Finish: Fourth
1987 Prediction: Fourth

Bruce Smith   **Jim Kelly**

The Bills took two important steps into the future by hiring Jim Kelly and Marv Levy last season. Kelly, who gets more than $1.5 million of owner Ralph Wilson's money every season, showed why he was the USFL's best over the second half last year. Levy, who gets paid much less, took over the coaching reins for the last seven games and showed why his organizational skills will help Kelly on his road to No. 1 in the NFL.

The Bills will not play in Super Bowl XXII. But they should improve on their 4–12 record a year ago (which improved on their 2–14 mark of the year before). Kelly, who seemed to throw key interceptions early in the year, tossed only five in the last eight games. With so-so help, he completed 59% of his passes for 3,593 yards and 22 TDs. Not a bad debut. But the running game, with unknown four-year vet Robb Riddick and some lesser-knowns, was awful. Fortunately, Kelly had a couple of decent receivers, like Andre Reed and TE Pete Metzelaars. They caught 53 and 49 passes, respectively.

Up front, tackles Joe Devlin and Tim Vogler and guards Jim Ritcher and Will Wolford should be back, though who will play which position may not be settled until opening day. Kent Hull should be the center.

DRE Bruce Smith, former No. 1 draft pick, anchors the up-and-coming defensive line. What the Bills' defense needs is speed, particularly from the secondary. The line, featuring vet NT Fred Smerlas and end Sean McNanie along with Smith, is okay.

The insertion of ex-USFLer Ray Bentley into the lineup at LILB helped the defense late in '86. He joins veterans Darryl Talley, Lucius Sanford, Eugene Marve, and No. 1 draftee Shane Conlan behind the line. Levy is a firm believer in helping your offense by building your defense. He's looking carefully for more backfield speed, where Charles Romes, Derrick Burroughs, Steve Freeman, Martin Bayless, and friends combined for only 10 interceptions during all of 1986.

Placekicker Scott Norwood made only three of 13 FG attempts from farther than 40 yards a year ago, not good enough by NFL standards.

AFC East
INDIANAPOLIS COLTS
1986 Finish: Fifth
1986 Prediction: Fifth

Bill Brooks

Duane Bickett

There are those who say that Colt coach
Ron Meyer and Colt owner Robert Irsay
deserve each other. (Still-smarting fans in
Baltimore feel that Irsay deserves worse.)
The two are hardly famous for winning
friends. But Meyer, one-time Patriot boss
and the 10th coach in Irsay's 15 years as
Colt owner, comes into '87 3–0, and how
many coaches can make that claim?

Meyer took over from Rod Dowhower late
last year with the club at 0–13, then knocked
off Atlanta, Buffalo, and the Raiders to
achieve his undefeated mark. Along the
way he reinstalled Gary Hogeboom as his
QB with outstanding results. Former starter
Jack Trudeau will still be heard from,
though he seems to lack Hogeboom's leadership qualities.

34

The receivers are certainly good enough, particularly last year's rookie WR Bill Brooks, whose 1,131 receiving yards place him third all-time among rookies. Matt Bouza, on the opposite side, is excellent, too. Two Pro Bowlers, C Ray Donaldson and LT Chris Hinton (who may move to LG), anchor the defensive front, which needs some beefing up. RG Ron Solt should be healthy again, which should help.

One of Mrs. Wonsley's many talented sons, George, should return at HB. FB Randy McMillan was seriously injured in a car accident. But the Colts' 1,491 rushing yards was the team's fewest in nearly two decades. Albert Bentley will be back.

There will be changes on defense, where Barry Krauss, longtime star LB, is a question mark following serious knee surgery. ROLB Duane Bickett, in only two years out of USC, is the defensive key, along with highly rated draftee Cornelius Bennett. Up front, it's second-year man Jon Hand trying to make an impact, along with NT Scott Kellar and vet DE Donnell Thompson. The Colts feature a mostly veteran secondary, with safeties Nesby Glasgow and Dwight Hicks and corners Leonard Coleman and Eugene Daniel.

Only Giant Sean Landeta does a better job than Colt punter Rohn Stark, the AFC Pro Bowler. Dean Biasucci faces a challenge to remain the Colts' placekicker in '87. Meyer may be tough enough to help this club, but there's a talent shortage.

AFC Central
CLEVELAND BROWNS
1986 Finish: First
1987 Prediction: First

Cody Risien

Bernie Kosar

Browns' coach Marty Schottenheimer should keep his doctor with him on the sidelines at all times. Seems that Cleveland lets just about every game come down to the final seconds. Good thing is that they win most of them.

The one they didn't win last year was the AFC title match. They should have. We believe they were the better team. They could well have given the Giants a tougher time in Super Bowl XXI.

One of the youngest top teams in the game, the Browns have an excellent shot at Supe XXII. Though slightly slow afoot, 23-year-old Bernie Kosar has proven himself a top pro QB. He hit on 58.4% of his passes a year ago, with 17 TD strikes.

The running game is excellent, and getting better. Ernest Byner was the team's leading rusher (94 for 277) and leading receiver before going down for the season. Cedric Mack picked up 665 yards; and ex-Colt Curtis Dickey, a waiver pickup, tossed in another 523. But the pass-receivers are even younger and better. Wideouts Webster Slaughter and Reggie Langhorne had 79 catches between them. Brian Brennan was the top man with 55 catches. None is more than 24 years old. Herman Fontenot (47 receptions) is tops out of the backfield. Still-tough Ozzie Newsome (39) may be nearing the end of his career.

There's plenty of strength up front with tackles Rickey Bolden and all-star Cody Risien, guards Paul Farren and Dan Fike, and center Mike Baab. There's good depth, too.

After some early problems, the Browns' defense caught up with the offense. All-Pro CB Hanford Dixon, possibly the finest pass-coverage back in the league, joins Frank Minnifield at the corners, with Ray Ellis (who replaced Al Gross) and Chris Rockins (who replaced the late Don Rogers) at the safeties. Top pick Mike Junkin joins OLB Clay Matthews. (Chip Banks is gone to San Diego.) Eddie Johnson and Anthony Griggs are the inside men.

Schottenheimer does plenty of platooning up front with Sam Clancy and Dave Puzzuoli helping ends Reggie Camp and Carl Hairston and noseman Bob Golic, who are great against the run.

AFC Central
PITTSBURGH STEELERS
1986 Finish: Third
1987 Prediction: Second

Bryan Hinkle   **Earnest Jackson**

If Earnest Jackson is for real, the Pittsburgh Steelers have a shot at continuing the comeback they began at midseason a year ago. Jackson always runs for big yardage, but rarely twice in a row for the same team.

The Steelers got off to a horrid 1–6 start in '86, with only an overtime win over lowly Houston to show for it. Over the last half, with Jackson keying the running game, they went 5–4. The four losses were by a total of 18 points, including overtimers to play-off-bound Cleveland and Chicago.

Still, Chuck Noll has plenty of work ahead. Jackson has beefed up the running game (910 yards in 13 games). Noll could concentrate on other areas in the draft. After a terrible start, Mark Malone finished fast and, at last, seems in charge of the Steeler offense. RB Walter Abercrombie was one of only three Pittsburgh offensive players to start all 16 games.

The receivers were especially banged up. When healthy, however, John Stallworth and Louis Lipps are among the best, and TE Preston Gothard is solid.

The offensive line also displayed plenty of improvement, despite an assortment of injuries. Only RG Terry Long was there every week. But C Mike Webster is a past All-Pro, tackles Tunch Ilkin and Ray Pinney are sound, and LG Craig Wolfley is an eight-year vet. It's a pretty decent group.

Defense is another story. While the front three are satisfactory (ends Keith Willis and Edmund Nelson; nose tackle and team captain Gary Dunn), there are big gaps among the linebackers and cornerbacks.

Pittsburgh's leading tackler, ROLB Bryan Hinkle is top-notch. But help is needed inside, where Robin Cole and David Little have been managing for years. Mike Merriweather should return to his usual spot on the left outside.

Top picks Rod Woodson and Delton Hall could move right in at the corners, where help is really needed. Vet Donnie Shell and Eric Williams should be back at the safeties.

Special teams are another Steeler concern. The 1986 specials gave up six TDs, costing the team at least three games. That simply will not do. Fortunately Noll has the smarts to turn things around.

AFC Central
CINCINNATI BENGALS
1986 Finish: Second
1987 Prediction: Third

Cris Collinsworth

Boomer Esiason

The only sure thing about the Bengal offense is that you can never be sure how well they'll play during a given game. That means, of course, that the Cincy defense has to be ready to dominate on those days — and it can't.

Cincinnati could overtake Cleveland for the AFC Central title. They haven't missed by much the last couple of years. But it will take a solid effort by all of the Bengals.

QB Boomer Esiason remains one of the NFL's future superstars. He's big, strong, and talented; he threw for 24 TDs last year. RB James Brooks has proven himself, off his club-record 163-yard (single game) and 1,087-yard (season) performances. He also caught passes for another 686 yards.

The receiving corps is in great shape.

Cris Collinsworth (62 catches for 1,024 yards) and Eddie Brown (58 for 964) are excellent, with young Tim McGee, a top kick-returner, ready to step in.

Up front, All-Pro Anthony Munoz is a tower of strength at LT, while RG Max Montoya is a Pro Bowler. C Dave Rimington, LG Bruce Kozerski, and RT Joe Walter round out the excellent quintet.

Some of the Cincinnati defensive failures are difficult to understand. The Bengals have drafted for defense in recent years, and some of the young people have come through. Nevertheless, it's a problem that coach Sam Wyche knows he will have to solve.

The secondary looks as if it's ready to become one of the AFC's best. Lewis Billups should be set for years at the right corner, with David Fulcher set at strong safety. Lewis Breeden remains a star at LCB. Rookies Eric Thomas and Leonard Bell could help.

Defensive ends Eddie Edwards and Ross Browner have seen better days, though they're still better than many. The Bengals made Brigham Young's Jason Buck their top draft pick for just this reason. They could also use a great linebacker.

It would surprise a lot of folks in Ohio to find Jeff Hayes back as the Bengal punter in '87. He was simply awful a year ago. Vet PK Jim Breech (17 of 32 field-goal tries) was no great shakes, either. Special teams are a major problem.

AFC Central
HOUSTON OILERS
1986 Finish: Fourth
1987 Prediction: Fourth

John Grimsley   **Ernest Givins**

After playing .500 ball over the last half
of 1986 and being blessed with a pair of
outstanding wide receivers, the Oilers enter
'87 with high hopes. They are probably too
high. Houston does too many dumb things
on the field — penalties, fumbles — to
really turn things around.

The hope springs from the new and
exciting passing game that blossomed after
Houston's awful 1–8 start last year. QB
Warren Moon begged coach Jerry Glanville for a shot at opening up the offense.
When Glanville agreed, Moon discovered
WRs Drew Hill, the ex-Ram, and Ernest
Givins, the touted rookie. The pair wound
up with 2,174 yards between them and gave
the Oilers a pair of 1,000-yard receivers for
only the second time in club history. TE

Jamie Williams is probably a better blocker than receiver. RB Mike Rozier (662 yards) also benefited from the offensive changes before going down with a knee injury with three weeks to go. Top pick Alonzo Highsmith should be a big hit.

The front five should improve if C Jim Romano and LG Mike Munchak return healthy from injured reserve. Bruce Mathews will be back at LT, along with RG Kent Hill and RT Dean Steinkuhler.

There's even more hope on defense, where the Oilers progressed from 27th in the league to 13th. DLE Ray Childress was outstanding in his second year, matched with DRE Richard Byrd. Doug Smith, healthy gain, should be back at NT.

After ousting Avon Riley from the starting job at LILB at midseason, John Grimsley went on to lead the team in tackles (199) and first-hits (112). Robert Lyles joins him on the left side, along with much-improved Johnny Meads on the right outside and Robert Abraham at RILB.

The Oilers' blitzing style of defense puts extra pressure on the cornerbacks, but only four opponents managed to complete as many as 50% of their passes against Houston. That's a credit to CBs Steve Brown and Patrick Allen. SS Keith Bostic was much improved, and Bo Eason should return at FS.

The Oiler defense, however, will have to cut down on its horrid totals of 39 TD passes allowed and its pitiful 32 sacks.

AFC West
SEATTLE SEAHAWKS
1986 Finish: Third
1987 Prediction: First

Dave Krieg   **Curt Warner**

Seattle starts '87 with an active five-game winning streak, the AFC's longest. A little consistency could produce an AFC West title.

The only NFL team to beat both Super Bowl entrants a year ago, the Seahawks were the hottest team in the league next to the Giants at the end of the '86 season. But they watched the play-offs on TV. Lots of AFC teams were relieved. QB Dave Krieg, who led the Seahawks to a league-high seven 30-point games a year ago — despite a midseason benching — will be back, throwing to future Hall of Famer Steve Largent and exciting Daryl Turner. Largent could become the NFL's all-time leading receiver by midseason.

The running game (fifth in the league last

year) is in excellent shape, with Curt Warner (319 carries for 1,481 yards, tops by a mile in the AFC) coming off his finest season and John L. Williams, last year's rookie flash who can run, block, and catch.

The revamped offensive line should improve, with tackles Ron Mattes and Mike Wilson, guards Bryan Millard and Edwin Bailey, and either Blair Bush or Will Grant (who replaced the injured Bush last year) at center.

Defense was one of the keys to last year's fast finish. The Seahawks allowed five fewer points per game during the last five games than during the season as a whole. DLE Jacob Green is one of the best. Joe Nash and Reggie Kinlaw will battle at NT, with No. 1 draftee Tony Woods ready to step in at DRE.

Linebacking is solid. LILB Fredd Young is a Pro Bowler, and joins Keith Butler inside and Bruce Scholtz and Greg Gaines on the outside. The linebackers are always Seattle's leading tacklers.

The return of regular All-Pro Kenny Easley at strong safety is a question mark. If he can't go, Paul Moyer will step in. FS Eugene Robinson will be back for a second starting year, along with veteran cornerback Dave Brown and young cornerback Terry Taylor. Watch for Kerry Justin and Patrick Hunter to see more action.

Placekicker Norm Johnson has great range, but punter Vince Gamache will have to improve on his rookie stats.

AFC West
LOS ANGELES RAIDERS
1986 Finish: Fourth
1987 Prediction: Second

Todd Christensen   **Bill Pickel**

When we picked the Raiders to go to the
last Super Bowl, we believed that owner Al
Davis would find someone to quarterback
the Silver and Black. We're still waiting. At
press time, the L.A. QBs were still named
Wilson and Plunkett, neither of whom is
likely to earn the Raiders a trip to Super
Bowl XXII. Add to that an aging offensive
line and a banged-up Marcus Allen, and
L.A. will need some magic to score big.

With Plunkett now 39 and Wilson operating under a cloud, the Raiders still talk
bravely about backup Rusty Hilger. We're
not convinced. Superback Allen nursed a
sprained ankle through much of '86 and
wound up with only 759 yards. Part-time
sailor, part-time runner Ensign Napoleon
McCallum (536 yards) may not be back in

'87 because of his Navy duties.

The AFC's best tight end, Todd Christensen (95 catches for 1,153 yards), is a key for any Raider passer, but the rest of the receivers, including Dokie Williams, Frank Hawkins, and Jessie Hester, are not up to Raider standards. Allen is a big threat coming out of the backfield.

The offensive line, taken for granted for too many years, is aging badly. Henry Lawrence finally had to sit last year, replaced by another old-timer, Shelby Jordan. Mickey Marvin, long the starter at RG, isn't a kid anymore. Only C Don Mosebar has a long future ahead. A healthy Curt Marsh would help.

Defensively there's plenty of strength up front, with super Howie Long at DLE and Bill Pickel at NG as good as any pair in the AFC. DRE Sean Jones has blossomed.

The M boys at linebacker, including LILB Matt Millen, RILB Reggie McKenzie, and ROLB Rod Martin, join LOLB Jerry Robinson.

CB Lester Hayes still has some years left at cornerback, though injuries forced him to the bench a year ago. Ex-receiver Sammy Seale filled in nicely. Mike Haynes is still excellent at the other corner. Stacy Toran and Vann McElroy should return at the safeties where both were most impressive.

The Raiders' veteran punter Ray Guy has announced his retirement, and that's all this club needs. Off four straight losses at the end of '86, the Raiders should begin '87 talking to themselves.

AFC West
DENVER BRONCOS
1986 Finish: First
1987 Prediction: Third

Dennis Smith   **John Elway**

Though the 1986 season wound up in Giant flames at the Rose Bowl last January, Denver has the tools for another Supe trip to San Diego this season.

Coach Dan Reeves still needs help with the running game. But the rest of the club is in great shape, especially the John-Elway-led passing attack. The ex-Stanford star is the kind of leader coaches love (280 for 504; 3,485 yards; 19 TDs). The 98-yard drive that beat the Browns in the AFC title game offers positive proof. Running backs Sammy Winder and Gerald Willhite (only 1,154 yards between them) are a little better than ordinary. The Broncs averaged only 3.7 yards per carry in '86. The receivers are excellent, led by wideouts Vance Johnson and Steve Watson, with top pick Ricky

Nattiel and little Mark Jackson ready to step in. Huge (6–5, 256-pound) Orson Mobley is a big surprise at tight end, where Clarence Kay may or may not bounce back.

The offensive line is steady, if not spectacular. Tackles Dave Studdard and Ken Lanier, guards Keith Bishop and Mark Cooper, and center Billy Bryan are probably better on pass protection than run-blocking.

There are questions about the defense, which allowed 37 points per game over the last five contests (play-offs included). Still, All-Pro DLE Rulon Jones is one of the AFC's best, and LILB Karl Mecklenburg is a sure-fire All-Pro. NT Greg Kragen and DRE Andre Townsend will likely join Jones up front, with LOLB Jim Ryan and RILB Ricky Hunley backing up the line. ROLB Tom Jackson's retirement surprised few in Denver. Simon Fletcher and Bruce Klosterman may fit into the starting lineup.

The corners are in fine shape, with Mike Harden coming off his best season. Louis Wright can still do it, but at age 34, his cornerback days may be limited. Free safety Steve Foley is now 33, but strong safety Dennis Smith is one of the best.

After three tries in '86, Denver may have found its punter of the future in Mike Horan. And despite a poor Super Bowl, place-kicker Rich Karlis is first-rate.

If coach Reeves can answer some of the key questions, the Broncos will be right in the thick of the AFC title race.

AFC West
KANSAS CITY CHIEFS
1986 Finish: Second
1987 Prediction: Fourth

Lloyd Burruss   **Bill Maas**

The headline in the Chiefs' 1986 post-season press guide reads: "K.C. completes most successful season in last 15." The NFL stats for '86 show the Chiefs' offense 28th in the 28-team league. So there are high expectations and a major problem as former special-teams coach Frank Gansz becomes the head man.

Start with a horrid running game that produced not one 100-yard game by any runner. (In the play-off clincher, Kaycee's offense failed to score a point.) The Chiefs' top two draft picks (RBs little Paul Palmer and huge Christian Okoye) should help. Gansz brought in UCLA offensive coordinator Homer Smith to handle that part of the game. He's a great one, but what can he do without a clearcut No. 1 QB (Bill Kenney or

Todd Blackledge)? He must pick one, and the choice isn't easy. Receiving is in decent shape, with last year's surprise Stephone Paige (52 for 829 yards) and Henry Marshall (46 for 652 yards). The return of Carlos Carson and Anthony Hancock will help.

Up front, there will be more changes. T Irv Eatman was a major disappointment a year ago, but LT David Lutz, guards Mark Adickes and Brad Budde, and center Rick Donnalley are fairly solid. Watch for young Brian Jozwiak to get considerably more time this season. The running backs? Who knows who'll be out there in '87.

The secondary is the key to the Chiefs' defense. (And how important is the defense to a play-off team that finishes last in offense?) There is no better safety combination in the league than SS Lloyd Burruss and FS Deron Cherry. Cherry is an All-Pro, and Burruss didn't miss by much. The corners are ably handled by Kevin Ross and Albert Lewis.

LILB Dino Hackett was one of the NFL rookie stars of '86 and should return, along with Louis Cooper on the left side and veteran Gary Spani and Tim Cofield on the right side.

Up front, there's lots of power with DLE Art Still still in the prime of his career, NT Bill Maas among the top two or three in the league, and former Bengal Pete Koch seemingly settled in on the right, though injured Mike Bell should be healthy enough to recapture the position.

AFC West
SAN DIEGO CHARGERS
1986 Finish: Fifth
1987 Prediction: Fifth

Gary Anderson

Billy Ray Smith

Thanks to the offensive firepower of QB Dan Fouts, the Chargers may be the scariest 4–12 team in the NFL. But new coach Al Saunders's 1987 play-off talk is probably quite premature.

Fouts, a 15-year veteran, is the No. 2 all-timer in passes and yardage in league history. He could have problems in '87, with Wes Chandler as his only experienced wide receiver. Trumaine Johnson and Timmy Ware will get plenty of action. Tight end is still well populated with a bunch of vets and top rookie Rob Bernstine.

But the all-everything guy in San Diego is Gary Anderson, who led the team in rushing (127 for 442 yards), receiving (80 catches), punt returns (25), and kickoff returns (24). Injuries played havoc with the rest of the Charger running game a year ago, with Curtis Adams, Lionel James, and Buford McGee (seven TDs in nine games) all missing a major chunk of the season.

Injuries also hurt the offensive line, where RG Dennis McKnight and RT Gary Kowalski were the only two every-game starters. C Don Macek is returning after a fine season, and LG Sam Claphan and LT Jim Lachey are first-rate.

Saunders emphasized defense when he replaced veteran coach Don Coryell midway through the 1986 season. That should pay long-term dividends for the Chargers. Still, San Diego needs help at every defensive position, though the healthy return of Leslie O'Neal would help the defensive line. End Lee Williams offers future hope, too. Terry Unrein and Chuck Ehin should return at NT, with Dee Hardison and Earl Wilson helping up front.

LOLB Billy Ray Smith is San Diego's defensive leader (11 sacks). LILB Gary Plummer, RILB Thomas Benson, and ROLB veteran Woodrow Lowe are all due back, and Chip Banks arrives from Cleveland. Watch for special teams expert Ty Allert to see more action, along with Andy Hawkins and healthy Derrie Nelson.

SS Jeff Dale returns after an outstanding season, with Gill Byrd ready to start at either free safety or cornerback. Vencie Glenn will start at free safety if Byrd is the cornerback. This team will get better, but not necessarily in 1987.

As the Falcons try to battle back in the NFC West, they start with a "huge" advantage: All-Pro guard Bill Fralic.

National
Football
Conference
Team Previews

NFC East
WASHINGTON REDSKINS
1986 Finish: Second
1987 Prediction: First

Jay Schroeder   **Art Monk**

The Redskins' goal for 1987 is to take that one giant step. Make it one *Giant* step. After three losses to the New Yorkers in '86, the 'Skins know what they have to do to undertake a trip to San Diego late next January.

Though the offense was shut out in the NFC title game, it's the defense that merits coach Joe Gibbs's attention. Linebackers Rich Milot, Neal Olkewicz, and Monte Coleman are all beginning to age. Tackle Dave Butz may or may not have another year left at age 36. Super end Dexter Manley must demonstrate that he has recovered from his off-field problems. He was the No. 2 sack specialist in the league. Linebacker Mel Kaufman must bounce back from achilles tendon problems but may never fully recover. Up front, Charles Mann and Darryl Grant are fine; and youngsters such as Dean Hamel, Steve Hamilton, and Markus Koch will get a shot.

In the secondary, Darrell Green at LCB is one of the NFL's best, but the other corner (Vernon Dean, Barry Wilburn) is a question. SS Alvin Walton had a fine rookie year, and Curtis Jordan set at FS.

Jay Schroeder, the "Mad Bomber," should be the Washington QB for years to come. He had 10 completions of more than 50 yards last season. His receiver corps is first-rate, led by tricky Art Monk and Gary Clark. They caught 147 passes between them last year. The backups, including Ricky Sanders and Clarence Verdin, have possibilities. The tight-end picture is somewhat clouded, though Don Warren and Clint Didier return.

There's a ton of experience up front, with tackles Joe Jacoby and Mark May, guards Russ Grimm and R.C. Thielemann, and center Joe Bostic. All except May have played in at least one Pro Bowl. Raleigh McKenzie will see plenty of action.

Despite a 1,203-yard season from George Rogers (including a league-high 18 TDs) and potential from injured Kelvin Bryant, the Redskins are looking for help at running back. Maybe ex-Maryland scoring star Rick Badanjek will fill the bill.

Punter Steve Cox is all set, but there will be a battle for the placekicker spot from last year's last two kickers, Jess Atkinson and Max Zendejas.

NFC East
NEW YORK GIANTS
1986 Finish: First
1987 Prediction: Second

Harry Carson   **Phil Simms**

There are folks in Chicago who insist that the Bears would have beaten the Giants in the NFC title game (had the Bears made it) and won their second straight Super Bowl. Forget it! For the Giants to repeat, however, they will have to do two things: Change the course of history (few NFL teams repeat) and continue to avoid injuries.

Given those two big *ifs*, the Giants have everything they need to repeat. The defense is incredibly tough. The linebackers are the best in the business, with the backup Giants good enough to start for almost anyone. ROLB Lawrence Taylor was the best in the game in '86, making LOLB Carl Banks even better. There are some concerns about RILB Harry Carson's age (33), but no doubts about LILB Gary Reasons nor backups Byron Hunt and Andy Headen. Up front, DLE George Martin returns for one more shot at age 34. DRE Leonard Marshall is super, and NT Jim Burt is amazingly tough. There's depth here, too, with Eric Dorsey, Erik Howard, and Jerome Sally.

If there's a weakness in the Giant defense, it's the secondary, where Mark Collins and Perry Williams man the corners with Terry Kinard and Kenny Hill at safety.

If there were ever any questions about QB Phil Simms, he answered them in the Super Bowl (22 of 25 pass completions). He has a great ability to hang in against fearsome rushes. He has accomplished it with a receiving corps that is suspect. The return of injured Lionel Manual helped; and Stacy Robinson, Bob Johnson, and Phil McConkey give it their best shot. No. 1 draftee Mark Ingram should fit right in. Mark Bavaro is the best TE in the NFL. Backup Zeke Mowatt could start for anyone else.

The offensive line, which finally jelled in '86, is led by tackles Brad Benson and Karl Nelson, guards Billy Ard and Chris Godfrey, and center Bart Oates. Damian Johnson and William Roberts provide good depth. And, of course, there's little Joe Morris, the exciting runner who makes the whole offense go. There's great blocking from Maurice Carthon, catching from Tony Galbreath, support from Ottis Anderson, and a 1987 return from George Adams. Add kicking (Sean Landeta and Raul Allegre) and you have a perfect shot at a repeat.

NFC East
DALLAS COWBOYS
1986 Finish: Third
1987 Prediction: Third

Herschel Walker   **Randy White**

Last year's losing season (7–9) was Dallas's first after 20 straight winners. Can coach Tom Landry end the streak right there? He'll have to do some fast shuffling to accomplish it.

Some are taking great joy in watching America's Team rebuild. Knowing the Cowboys' leadership, their joy may be short-lived. Having Herschel Walker from Day 1, and finding a permanent spot for the USFL star, who gained 737 yards on the ground, caught 76 passes for 837 yards, and scored 14 TDs, is bound to help. Of course, Tony Dorsett is still as dangerous as ever.

Interestingly, the Cowboy offense went to sleep after a fractured wrist sidelined QB Danny White in game nine. His return will help. Backup Steve Pelleur just didn't get the job done, and Reggie Collier doesn't appear ready. Tony Hill will have to bounce back from a so-so season, but last year's rookie star Mike Sherrard gives the Cowboys a deep threat that had been missing.

Up front, RT Phil Pozderac will have to overcome the holding-penalty disease that plagued him last season. There may have to be other changes in the unit that features tackle Mark Tuinei, guards Crawford Ker and Glen Titensor, and center Tom Rafferty. TE Doug Cosbie is first-rate.

Defensively the Cowboys failed to put much pressure on opposing quarterbacks, and the secondary failed to come up with the big play. The front four — ends Too Tall Jones and Jim Jeffcoat, tackles John Dutton and Randy White — have been together a long while. Rookie Danny Noonan could help. The linebackers are satisfactory, if not better. Mike Hegman is set on the left side, with Eugene Lockhart in the middle and Jeff Rohrer on the right. Look for Steve DeOssie and either Garth Jax or Jessie Penn to get a shot in '87.

The disappointment for Landry is that his secondary has made the big play in the past. Corners Everson Walls and Ron Fellows are exciting players, and no one hits as hard as SS Bill Bates. FS Michael Downs can get the job done. The turnaround can begin here.

With PK Rafael Septien gone, the kicking game is in doubt.

NFC East
PHILADELPHIA EAGLES
1986 Finish: Fourth
1987 Prediction: Fourth

Reggie White

Randall Cunningham

If talk is cheap, don't blame the phone company. Send the bill to Eagles' coach Buddy Ryan. Buddy talked a good game last year, but his team did not make good on his words. Now he's talking play-offs in '87 and Super Bowl in '88, and neither seems likely. Still, Eagle owner Norman Braman is banking on Buddy's words, and failures could cause problems.

There's some talent, of course, QB Randall Cunningham remains an exciting threat — when he's not flat on his back. He threw for eight TDs and ran for five more. Trouble is, he was sacked 72 times. He may be getting some help in the running department, where Keith Byars and Anthony Toney show signs of promise.

There's talent in the receiving department,

too. WR Mike Quick is one of the best (60 catches, 939 yards), and Kenny Jackson and Greg Garrity can get the job done. TE John Spagnola is tough, and RB Junior Tautalatasi is excellent coming out of the backfield.

Up front, C Gerry Feehery should be back from injured reserve, with rookie ace Matt Darwin playing behind him. Tackles Ken Reeves and Joe Conwell and guards Bob Landsee and Ron Baker will have to do a better job protecting Cunningham.

On defense, left end Reggie White is one of those great impact players. He had 16 sacks in the last nine games after moving over from tackle. Obviously Ryan's 46 defense lacked something in coming over from Chicago. (What it lacked, of course, was the Bears' defensive players.) Look for Greg Brown to rejoin White at end, with Ken Clarke and Clyde Simmons back at the tackles. Top rookie Jerome Brown, an All-America at Miami U., could also fit right in at tackle. Garry Cobb could see more action backing up starting linebackers Seth Joyner, Mike Reichenbach, and Alonzo Johnson.

The defensive key could come in the healthy return of FS Wes Hopkins, perhaps the Eagles' best player, who missed the last 12 games. Roynell Young and Elbert Foules should return at the corners, with Andre Waters at strong safety.

The kicking game is in sorry shape. PK Paul McFadden missed 11 of 31 FGs in '86.

NFC East
ST. LOUIS CARDINALS
1986 Finish: Fifth
1987 Prediction: Fifth

Leonard Smith   **J.T. Smith**

When owner Bill Bidwill threatens, as he often does, to move the Cardinals, many St. Louisans these days are prone to say, "Go!" The (not-so) Big Red seem years away from catching the more talented teams in the NFC East, probably the toughest division in the NFL.

Coach Gene Stallings has problems everywhere. His club suffered through a bunch of injuries (Pat Tilley, Curtis Greer, Benny Perrin, Roy Green, and E.J. Junior, among others) last year. And he played with one of the youngest lineups this side of *Mr. Rogers' Neighborhood*.

Stallings will likely give Neil Lomax another shot at the QB spot. The one-time QB of the Future (after a 4,600-yard season in '84) nearly became the QB of the Past when Cliff Stoudt replaced him at midyear. Lomax is back now, but for how long? Will No. 1 draftee Kelly Stouffer be the long-range QB answer? RB Stump Mitchell finally took over from O.J. Anderson (gone to the Giants), getting a chance to prove that his 5.2-yard-per-carry average was no fluke. Earl Ferrell runs with Mitchell, with Ron Wolfley ready in short-yardage situations. If Green and Tilley are at full speed, the receiver corps will be much improved. Their injuries allowed veteran J.T. Smith to become a top threat (a team-record 80 catches for 1,014 yards). TE Doug Marsh will have to increase his production.

The offensive line — including tackles Luis Sharpe and Tootie Robbins, guards Doug Dawson and Joe Bostic, and center Gene Chilton — should be healthy and ready to go.

Stallings is thinking about switching from a 3–4 to a 4–3 defense. His linebackers, E.J. Junior, Freddie Joe Nunn, and Anthony Bell, were a major disappointment a year ago (no interceptions, only two fumble recoveries). There will be hot competition for the up-front jobs, with last year's regulars, Bob Clasby, David Galloway, and Al Baker, trying to hold off Stafford Mays, Mark Duda, and the returning Curtis Greer.

SS Leonard Smith is the keystone in the secondary. He's one of the NFL's best. Lonnie Young is the free safety with Carl Carter, Cedric Mack, and Wayne Smith at the corners.

NFC Central
CHICAGO BEARS
1986 Finish: First
1987 Prediction: First

Mark Bortz   **Walter Payton**

Outside of quarterback, the Bears are a team without an obvious weakness. There are All-Pros and Pro Bowlers, future Pro Bowlers and past Pro Bowlers at nearly every key position. And these fellows are proven winners with a coach who has won nearly seven of every 10 games during his career.

But that single question mark, the quarterback, overrides all of the pluses in evaluating this team.

Will QB Jim McMahon recover from shoulder surgery in time for the '87 season? Will he ever fully recover? If he recovers, can he and coach Mike Ditka work together? Can the Bears win with Mike Tomczak? Doug Flutie? Steve Fuller? Rookie Jim Harbaugh? Someone else? The answer is: With all of the above, the Bears went 14–2 in '86. No Giant fans were upset when the Bears lost to the Redskins in the NFC semifinals.

Basically this club is loaded. Walter Payton (1,333 yards) is just stopping in Chicago on his way to the Hall of Fame in Canton, OH. And youngsters like Thomas Sanders and Neal Anderson look as if they can step in anytime. FB Matt Suhey is one of those blue-collar, hard workers who gets his job done. Receivers Willie Gault, Keith Ortego (say *ORT*-e-go), and Dennis Gentry are good enough, as is TE Emery Moorehead. The front five is outstanding, particularly on the left side where Jim Covert and Mark Bortz hang out. Add C Jay Hilgenberg, RG Tom Thayer, and RT Keith Van Horne, and you've got quite a group.

The defense is outstanding, particularly if huge RT Fridge Perry bounces back. LE Dan Hampton, LT Steve McMichael, and RE Richard Dent are All-Pros. The LBs are even better. Try to spot a weakness in Otis Wilson, Mike Singletary, and Wilber Marshall. Only Wilson failed to make our All-Pro team, and not by much.

There may be some reservations about the secondary; but safeties Dave Duerson and Gary Fencik are the toughest hitters in the game, and Mike Richardson and Vestee Jackson are just fine, thank you, on the corners.

With or without a star QB, the Bears will be in the Super Bowl hunt next January.

NFC Central
MINNESOTA VKINGS
1986 Finish: Second
1987 Prediction: Second

Joey Browner   **Tommy Kramer**

The Vikings came within a whisker of making the 1986 play-offs. (Their loss to the Oilers will haunt them forever.) Now, however, they are a team which *should* make the play-offs — which will make the job harder.

Thanks to a super season from Tommy Kramer, the NFL's top-rated QB, the Vikes set and tied several club offensive records, including most points (398). If they can keep Kramer healthy, the play-offs are a real possibility this time around. Catching the Bears for the division title may take a little longer.

Minny chose Penn State's D.J. Dozier to join RBs Alfred Anderson and Darrin Nelson, the '86 workhorses. Five Vikings caught passes for more than 500 yards, led by TE Steve Jordan (859). RB Nelson joined the group, as did the three wide receivers, Anthony Carter (686), Leo Lewis (600), and Hassan Jones (570). It's a fine group.

Ex-USFL star Gary Zimmerman, who decided he didn't want to join the New York Giants (wrong year to make that choice!), gave great strength to the Viking offensive line from his spot at left tackle. That helped improve RT Tim Irwin, guards Jim Hough and Terry Tausch, and center Dennis Swilley. Coach Jerry Burns is ready to go with the same people again.

The defense is fairly strong, too, especially when the players are healthy. Mark Mullaney and Doug Martin both missed some time in '86, which hurt the pass-rush. Martin, brother of the Giants' George, will be back at the family position (left end) with Tim Newton and Keith Millard at the tackles and Chris Doleman at right end.

Though 12th-round draft pick Jesse Solomon was a major pleasant surprise last year, Scott Studwell may hold onto his MLB spot awhile longer. Chris Martin and David Howard start on the outside.

Burns admits he needs help in the secondary, where SS Joey Browner went on to the Pro Bowl. John Harris will open at FS, with Issiac Holt and Carl Lee penciled in at the corners.

Chuck Nelson, who had failed in two prior pro chances, firmly replaced PK Jan Stenerud, and Greg Coleman is a top-notch punter.

NFC Central
GREEN BAY PACKERS
1986 Finish: Fourth
1987 Prediction: Third

Mark Lee   **Randy Wright**

In Green Bay, where coach Forrest Gregg is still looking for his first winning season, the heat (regardless of the weather) is on. If the future is now, it appears fairly bleak.

It does look as if Gregg has found the QB of the future in Randy Wright. Over the second half of last season, Wright was simply brilliant. His ability to move is the key to his success, and that's not bad. His season totals (263 completions, 3,247 yards) were the third best in Packer history.

Offensively the major problem is the running game. Neither Kenneth Davis nor Gary Ellerson ever got untracked last year, leaving fullback-type Gerry Ellis to finish at RB. Auburn's Brent Fullwood, the Pack's top draftee, should be able to step right in at running back. He's first-rate.

Replacing James Lofton at WR won't be easy for Gregg. But young Walter Stanley was a pleasant surprise a year ago, and he'll likely join Eddie Lee Ivery. Veteran Dan Ross should return at TE.

Up front, Ken Ruettgers is set (for many years?) at left tackle, possibly the key spot on the line. He was one of the few tackles in the league to shut down Lawrence Taylor a year ago. The rest of the bunch, including tackle Alan Veingrad, guards Tom Neville and Ron Hallstrom, and center Karl Swanke, is fair.

The pass-rush all but disappeared last season. That puts extra pressure on ends Alphonso Carreker and Robert Brown and nosemen Charles (I hate Jim McMahon) Martin and Robert Brown.

The Pack is looking to RILB Brian Noble to anchor the linebacking group. The return of John Anderson will help the remaining starters, LOLB Robert Brown, LILB Randy Scott, and ROLB Bobby Leopold.

There's no question about the No. 1 defender in Green Bay. It's left cornerback Mark Lee. He had nine intercepts last season and did the job week-in and week-out. Last year's RCB Mossy Cade had some off-field problems. Tiger Greene and Ken Stills could return at the safeties.

PK Al Del Greco, who has made his last 63 extra points, should return. But the rest of the club is extremely young and in need of extra assistance.

NFC Central
DETROIT LIONS
1986 Finish: Third
1987 Prediction: Fourth

James Jones

Lomas Brown

The Detroit Lions, who could hardly lose at home in '85, went 1–7 at the Silverdome in '86. That sealed their fate — 5–11, their 12th losing season in the last 14. They should make it 13 of 15 in 1987.

Sure there's hope. A little. Chuck Long, the former Iowa All-America, is the quarterback of the future. His first NFL completion was a 34-yard TD strike. But whether that future comes in 1987 is another story. Or will it be another year of the much-booed Eric Hipple or Joe Ferguson?

Whoever the QB is will need some help in the receiver corps. WR Jeff Chadwick (53 catches for 995 yards) is a comer, but there isn't much help there.

The running game is in somewhat better shape. FB James Jones (252 carries, 903 yards) was voted the team's MVP for the third straight year, and RB Garry James (161 carries, 688 yards) is a top-notch companion. Special teams expert Herman Hunter and rookie Scott Williams provide excellent depth.

The offensive line should be better than it is. Despite missing four games, new RG Keith Dorney was outstanding, as usual. The rest of the crew, tackles Lomas Brown and Rich Strenger, ex-Oiler LG Harvey Salem, and C Steve Mott, must do a better job in '87 for the club to improve.

But the real problems are on defense. Coach Darryl Rogers needs better work in stopping the run, which may mean new faces at nose tackle and inside linebacker. There are no complaints, however, about young linebackers Mike Cofer and Jimmy Williams, returning from the injured list. Angelo King may join Cofer on the outside, with Vernon Maxwell and James Harrell competing in the middle. Up front, ends Keith Ferguson and William Gay have to crank up the pass-rush, and noseman Eric Williams has to learn how to stuff the run. Reggie Rogers, the top draft pick, should fit right in.

There's less concern about the secondary where Devon Mitchell made a major impact at free safety as a rookie last year. Vet Bruce McNorton and young Duane Galloway could return at the corners, with Demetrious Johnson scheduled again at strong safety.

NFC Central
TAMPA BAY BUCCANEERS
1986 Finish: Fifth
1987 Prediction: Fifth

Calvin Magee

Donald Igwebuike

Following another 2–14 season, the Bucs have decided to start from scratch. (Not a bad idea.) The scratch, slang for cash, belongs to owner Hugh Culverhouse, and he parted with a Brinks truckful to revamp his coaching staff and his offense.

The first blockbuster involved Ray Perkins. The one-time Giant coach (who began the New York rebuilding that led to the Super Bowl) left one of the highest-paying college jobs (U. of Alabama) to assume the Tampa Bay challenge.

Next Perkins spent whatever money Culverhouse had left to sign Miami U. QB Vinny Testaverde to a long-term contract. At $1.6 million per year, Testaverde will be expected to produce soon. Interestingly, when Perkins made Phil Simms the Giants'

No. 1 pick, he kept him on the bench until the New York fans and press hollered.

The quarterback, whoever he is, will get help from top-flight FB James Wilder. Things could be even better if Nathan Wonsley can, somehow, bounce back from a serious neck injury. The receiver corps, redone last year with the departure of Kevin House and Jimmie Giles, will rely on Vince Heflin, Gerald Carter, TE Calvin Magee, and anyone else Perkins can find.

Sean (I want out of Tampa) Farrell is out (gone to New England), leaving tackles Rob Taylor and Ron Heller, guard George Yarno, and center Randy Grimes.

The Bucs' defensive numbers boggle the mind. No Buc opponent scored fewer than 20 points last season, a stat that does not inspire confidence. DLE John Cannon will return, which helps. DRE Ron Holmes has plenty of room for improvement. The LBs, like Jackie Walker, Jeff Davis, Scot Brantley, Chris Washington, Keith Browner, and Ervin Randle, are okay and not a drop more. Many were high draft picks who haven't proven their worth. There are similar questions to be answered about the secondary, particularly about SS Craig Swoope and RCB Rod Jones. Craig Curry and Vito McKeever, along with Jeremiah Castille, are the returnees.

Possibly Tampa Bay's best last year was PK Donald Igwebuike, who hit on 17 of 24 field-goal attempts, missing nothing shorter than 37 yards.

NFC West
LOS ANGELES RAMS
1986 Finish: Second
1987 Prediction: First

Carl Ekern   Doug Smith

In Los Angeles (well, Anaheim, actually),
the present is Dickerson, the future is
Everett, and the outlook is positively rosy.
Rock-solid Eric Dickerson makes the Rams'
running game awesome. Promising Jim
Everett can't help but improve the Rams'
passing game (last in the league each of
the last two years). And with one of the best
defenses in the NFL, the Rams are, real-
istically, thinking Super Bowl.

Why not? Blessed with great coaching
from John Robinson, the Rams know what
they're about on the field. Mainly that
means giving the ball to Dickerson. The ex-
SMU star rushed for 1,821 yards last season, the sixth-best season in league history. Look at it this way: The 1,800-yard
barrier has been crashed only eight times

ever. Dickerson has done it three times —
in only four seasons! His RB partner Barry
Redden isn't bad, either.

The big hope is the passing game. The
Rams paid big for Everett, the ex-Purdue
star, but the gamble looks worthwhile. He
was most impressive against Dallas in a
TV game in December. He'll look for Henry
Ellard, a 1986 holdout who didn't catch his
first pass until Game 10 — yet wound up
the Rams' leading receiver. The line is
solid, featuring All-Pro RG Dennis Harrah, along with vet tackles Irv Pankey and
Jackie Slater, rookie stickout G Tom New-
berry, and C Doug Smith.

The defense is in fine shape. Doug Reed,
Shawn Miller, and Reggie Doss will start
again up front, with help from Gary Jeter
and Greg Meisner. Charlie DeJurnett should
return, too. The linebackers, led by RILB
Carl Ekern, are more than good enough.
Mark Jerue joins Ekern on the inside, while
veterans Mel Owens and Mike Wilcher man
the outside. Jim Collins and Steve Busick
return from injuries.

The secondary is tremendous. LeRoy
Irvin on the right corner is our All-Pro
choice. Jerry Gray, the LCB, stepped in to
replace Gary Green last year, then led the
Rams in interceptions with eight. The
safeties are a veteran bunch, with Vince
Newsome and Nolan Cromwell backed by
Johnnie Johnson and Tim Fox.

P Dale Hatcher's average slipped from
43.2 to 38.6 yards per punt last year.

NFC West
NEW ORLEANS SAINTS
1986 Finish: Fourth
1987 Prediction: Second

Rickey Jackson

Rueben Mayes

Coach Jim Mora isn't accustomed to losing. In the USFL, his Philadelphia/Baltimore Stars won back-to-back championships. Thus, while most of New Orleans was pleased with the team's flying 7–9 finish a year ago, Mora wasn't. Look for his club to do even better in '87.

There is the running game, of course. Rueben Mayes, the 13th running back selected in the 1986 draft, didn't start until the fifth Saint game. By the end of game 16, however, he had picked up 1,353 yards on 286 carries, a spectacular 4.7 yards per carry. And he did it on a bad achilles tendon that required postseason surgery. He's a winner. His backup Dalton Hilliard, the previous starter, isn't bad, either.

Things are not as promising for the

Saints' passing game. Q Bobby Hebert was doing all right — but barely — before going down with a broken foot. His replacement Dave Wilson was a hair better, but not much. Mora likes Wilson's attitude, which makes up for his lack of movement and passing distance.

When a runner picks up 4.7 yards per carry, you can usually look to his line. Despite injuries to top draftee Jim Dombrowski (another broken foot), Brad Edelman, and Ralph Williams, the line hung in. Credit Joel Hilgenberg, Chuck Commiskey, Bill Contz, and Stan Brock. Tight ends Hoby Brenner and John Tice are better blockers than receivers.

The defensive line needs help, but not much. If DLE Bruce Clark bounces back from knee surgery, so much the better. Tony Elliott and Jim Wilks were decent in the middle, with pass-rushing James Geathers and Frank Warren finishing well. The return of Casey Merrill will help.

LOLB Rickey Jackson is Pro Bowl quality, while ROLB James Haynes is steady. The rest of the crew, including Alvin Toles, Vaughan Johnson, Sam Mills, and Jack Del Rio, is okay. LCB Dave Waymer comes off his best year (nine interceptions). RCB Johnnie Poe was inconsistent and must improve. FS Frank Wattelet surprised some folks, while Antonio Gibson did well.

Special teams are a New Orleans highlight, with Morten Andersen the Pro Bowl PK and Mel Gray a first-rate KR.

NFC West
SAN FRANCISCO 49ERS
1986 Finish: First
1987 Prediction: Third

Ronnie Lott   **Joe Montana**

Can you isolate any 60 minutes of football and hang a label on a team? Usually you can't. But the 49–3 play-off pasting the Niners suffered against the Giants last January may set the tone for 1987.

When you consider that San Francisco led the same Giants 17–0 at halftime of a Monday night game in December before losing 21–17, the champs outscored the 49ers 70–3 over a game-and-a-half. That speaks volumes about coach Bill Walsh's ancient offensive line and doesn't say much about the defense, either.

Joe Montana made a memorable comeback from back surgery that could have ended his career last season. If he can't go, ex-Buc Steve Young is more than ready. Either QB has the NFL's top deep threat,

Jerry Rice, to throw to. That makes the rest of the receivers, Dwight Clark, TE Russ Francis, and others, even better. A hip injury limited super RB Roger Craig to only 830 yards last year. Backup Joe Cribbs (590 yards) sparkled late.

It's the line that's in trouble, however. RT Keith Fahnhorst is 35, RG Randy Cross is 33, C Fred Quillan is 31, and LG John Ayers is 34. Look for major changes in the next year or two. Only Cross and T Bubba Paris seem safe. Rookie Harris Barton should start soon.

Coach Walsh has begun to phase in some new talent on defense, with DE Charles Haley and Larry Roberts having impressed as rookies. Kevin Fagan may never come back from a bum knee, and John Harty is a long-term question mark. Dwaine Board and Manu Tuiasosopo are showing their age.

The linebackers are so-so. ROLB Keena Turner is an outstanding athlete, and LOLB Milt McColl really impressed in place of oft-injured Todd Shell. Inside, Riki Ellison and Jim Fahnhorst usually get the job done.

The one-time solid secondary still features the supreme Ronnie Lott at free safety. He had 10 interceptions last season, returning one for a TD against Green Bay after suffering a hairline leg fracture. CBs Tim McKyer and Don Griffin both played well as rookies, and Carlton Williamson remains one of the best strong safeties anywhere.

81

NFC West
ATLANTA FALCONS
1986 Finish: Third
1987 Prediction: Fourth

Gerald Riggs   **Mike Kenn**

We hear they had a contest in Atlanta last winter. First prize was a pair of tickets to a Falcon game. Second prize was the head coaching job. The second-prize winner was Marion Campbell, who inherits this confused club. Campbell had the job once before; he was fired 11 years ago. Now, with Dan Henning gone and some turndowns from a variety of college and pro coaches, it's Campbell's title again. It won't be any easier this time.

The quarterback picture is muddled. Neither David Archer nor Turk Schoenert could do the job last year. Chris Miller, the No. 1 draft pick, could see action soon. The receiver corps isn't much better. Charlie Brown was fairly consistent. He grabbed 63 passes for 918 yards.

The running game, spelled Gerald Riggs, seems in much better shape. The versatile Riggs carried 343 punishing times, picked up 1,327 yards, and scored nine rushing touchdowns. When you understand that quarterback Archer was the second-leading rusher with 298 yards, you get a better idea of Riggs's major role.

Good health will help restore the offensive line, which lost RT Brett Miller, LG John Scully, and LT Mike Kenn (a Pro Bowl fixture) for all or part of last season. Whether he's at guard (his best position) or tackle (where he was forced to play), big Bill Fralic is an All-Pro. He does the job every week and has become a solid leader.

Campbell's influence, a couple of trades, and some adjustments helped the Atlanta defense last year. That shouldn't change now that Campbell is the boss.

Best adjustment was made by RCB Scott Case, who moved over from safety. He picked off four passes, defensed 41 passes (double Bobby Butler's 1985 standard), and became one of the league's best corners. S Bret Clark did well after coming over from the Raiders.

There's strength up front with Mike Gann and Rick Bryan on the outside of draft star Tony Casillas. The linebackers are fairly secure, with Reggie Wilkes and Joel Williams playing outside of Buddy Curry and John Rade.

Veteran Mick Luckhurst will battle Ali Haji-Sheikh for the PK job.

Has St. Louis QB Neil Lomax had it? That was the Cards' message when they drafted Kelly Stouffer in the first round.

1987
NFL
Draft List

The following abbreviations are used to identify the players' positions:

OFFENSE: T = tackle; G = guard; C = center; QB = quarterback; RB = running back; WR = wide receiver; TE = tight end.

DEFENSE: DE = defensive end; DT = defensive tackle; LB = linebacker; DB = defensive back.

SPECIAL TEAMS: P = punter; K = placekicker.

The number preceding the player's name indicates the overall position in which he was drafted.

Atlanta Falcons
13. Chris Miller, QB, Oregon; 31. Kenny Flowers, RB, Clemson; 97. Ralph Van Dyke, T, So. Illinois; 125. Mike Mraz, DE, Utah State; 153. Paul Kiser, G, Wake Forest; 181. Michael Reid, LB, Wisconsin; 208. Curtis Taliaferro, LB, Va. Tech; 236. Terrence Anthony, DB, Iowa St.; 264. Jerry Reese, TE, Illinois; 292. Elbert Shelley, DB, Arkansas St.; 320. Larry Emery, RB, Wisconsin.

Buffalo Bills
8. Shane Conlan, LB, Penn State; 29. Nate Odomes, DB, Wisconsin; 33. Roland Mitchell, DB, Texas Tech; 60. David Brandon, LB, Memphis St.; 78. Jamie Mueller, RB, Benedictine; 108. Leon Seals, DT, Jackson St.; 171. Kerry Porter, RB, Washington St.; 209. Bruce Mesner, DT, Maryland; 227. Keith McKeller, TE, Jacksonville St.; 284. Howard Ballard, T, Alabama A&M; 311. Joe McGrail, DT, Delaware.

Chicago Bears
26. Jim Harbaugh, QB, Michigan; 54. Ron Morris, WR, SMU; 101. Sean Smith, DE, Grambling; 120. Steve Bryan, DE, Oklahoma; 138. Will Johnson, DE, NE Louisiana; 154. John Adickes, C, Baylor; 193. Archie Harris, OT, William & Mary; 221. Paul Magliazzo, LB, Oklahoma; 249. Lakei Heimull, Brigham Young; 277. Dick Chapura, DT, Missouri; 305. Tim Jessie, WR, Auburn; 333. Eric Jeffries, DB, Texas.

Cincinnati Bengals
17. Jason Buck, DE, Brigham Young; 49. Eric Thomas, DB, Tulane; 76. Leonard Bell, DB, Indiana; 77. Skip McClendon, DE, Arizona St.; 103. Jim Riggs, TE, Clemson; 130. Marc Logan, RB, Kentucky; 139. Greg Horn, P, Arkansas; 157. Sonny Gordon, DB, Ohio St.; 188. Chris Thatcher, G, Lafayette; 215. Solomon Wilcots, DB, Colorado; 242. Craig Raddatz, LB, Wisconsin; 269. David McCluskey, RB, Georgia; 296. Jim Warne, T, Arizona St.; 328. Jim Holifield, RB, West Virginia.

Cleveland Browns
5. Mike Junkin, LB, Duke; 32. Greg Rakoczy, C, Miami; 80. Tim Manoa, RB, Penn State; 82. Jeff Jaeger, K, Washington; 165. Stephen Braggs, DB, Clemson; 220. Steve Bullitt, LB, Texas A&M; 276. Frank Winters, C, Western Illinois; 303. Larry Brewton, DB, Temple.

Dallas Cowboys

12. Danny Noonan, DT, Nebraska; 39. Ron Francis, DB, Baylor; 68. Jeff Zimmerman, G, Florida; 95. Kelvin Martin, WR, Boston College; 124. Everett Gay, WR, Texas; 151. Joe Onosai, T, Hawaii; 180. Kevin Sweeney, QB, Fresno St.; 206. Kevin Gogan, T, Washington; 235. Alvin Blount, RB, Maryland; 262. Dale Jones, LB, Tennessee; 291. Jeff Ward, K, Texas; 318. Scott Armstrong, LB, Florida.

Denver Broncos

27. Rocky Nattiel, WR, Florida; 83. Michael Brooks, LB, LSU; 111. Marc Munford, LB, Nebraska; 167. Warren Marshall, RB, James Madison; 194. Wilbur Strozier, T, Georgia; 222. Dan Morgan, G, Penn State; 250. Bruce Plummer, DB, Mississippi St.; 278. Rafe Wilkerson, LB, Richmond; 299. Steve Roberts, DE, Washington; 306. Tommy Neal, RB, Maryland; 334. Tyrone Braxton, DB, No. Dakota St.

Detroit Lions

7. Reggie Rogers, DE, Washington; 63. Jerry Ball, DT, SMU; 92. Garland Rivers, DB, Michigan; 148. Danny Lockett, LB, Arizona; 175. Dan Saleaumua, DT, Arizona St.; 203. Dennis Gibson, LB, Iowa St.; 230. Rick Calhoun, RB, Fullerton St.; 259. Raynard Brown, WR, South Carolina; 286. Brian Siverling, TE, Penn State; 315. Gary Lee, WR, Georgia Tech.

Green Bay Packers

4. Brent Fullwood, RB, Auburn; 41. Johnny Holland, LB, Texas A&M; 61. David Croston, T, Iowa; 69. Scott Stephen, LB, Arizona St.; 71. Frankie Neal, WR, Ft. Hays St.; 88. Lorenzo Freeman, DT, Pittsburgh; 145. Willie Marshall, WR, Temple; 172. Tony Leiker, DT, Stanford; 191. Bill Smith, P, Mississippi; 198. Jeff Drost, DT, Iowa; 228. Gregg Harris, G, Wake Forest; 255. Don Majkowski, QB, Virginia; 282. Patrick Scott, WR, Grambling; 335. Norman Jefferson, DB, LSU.

Houston Oilers

3. Alonzo Highsmith, RB, Miami; 20. Haywood Jeffries, WR, No. Carolina St.; 46. Walter Johnson, LB, LSU; 64. Cody Carlson, QB, Baylor; 105. Mark Dusbabek, LB, Minnesota; 133. Spencer Tillman, RB, Oklahoma; 147. Al Smith, LB, Utah St.; 159. Toby Caston, LB, LSU; 176. Robert Banks, LB, Notre Dame; 202. Michel James, WR, Washington St.; 231. Wes Neighbors, C, Alabama; 258. Curtis Duncan, WR, Northwestern; 287. John Davis, G, Georgia Tech; 314. Ira Valentine, RB, Texas A&M.

Indianapolis Colts

2. Cornelius Bennett, LB, Alabama; 58. Chris Gambol, T, Iowa; 86. Randy Dixon, T, Pittsburgh; 114. Roy Banks, WR, Eastern Illinois; 142. Freddie Robinson, DB, Alabama; 170. Mark Bellini, WR, Brigham Young; 200. Chuckie Miller, DB, UCLA; 247. Bob Ontko, LB, Penn St.; 253. Chris Goode, DB, Alabama; 281. Jim Reynosa, DE, Arizona St.; 309. David Adams, RB, Arizona.

Kansas City Chiefs

19. Paul Palmer, RB, Temple; 35. Christian Okoye, RB, Azusa Pacific; 73. Todd Howard, LB, Texas A&M; 128. Kitrick Taylor, WR, Washington St.; 186. Doug Hudson, QB, Nicholls St.; 218. Michael Clemson, RB, William & Mary; 244. Randy Watts, DE, Catawba; 271. James Evans, RB, Southern; 298. Craig Richardson, WR, Eastern Washington; 325. Bruce Holmes, LB, Minnesota.

Los Angeles Raiders

15. John Clay, T, Missouri; 52. Bruce Wilkerson, T, Tennessee; 81. Steve Smith, RB, Penn State; 110. Steve Beuerlein, QB, Notre Dame; 183. Bo Jackson, RB, Auburn; 238. Scott Eccles, TE, Eastern New Mexico; 254. Rob Harrison, RB, Sacramento St.; 265. John Gesek, T, Sacramento St.; 273. Jim Ellis, LB, Boise St; 288. Chris McLemore, RB, Arizona; 294. Mario Perry, TE, Mississippi.

Los Angeles Rams

47. Donald Evans, DT, Winston-Salem; 74. Clifford Hicks, DB, Oregon; 91. Doug Bartlett, DE, Northern Illinois; 109. Larry Kelm, LB, Texas A&M; 136. Scott Mersereau, DT, So. Connecticut; 166. Jon Embree, TE, Colorado; 213. Michael Stewart, DB, Fresno St.; 240. Tracy Ham, RB, Georgia Southern; 272. David Smith, LB, Northern Arizona; 326. Alonzo Williams, Mesa; 332. Fred Stokes, DE, Georgia Southern.

Miami Dolphins

16. John Bosa, DE, Boston College; 43. Rick Graf, LB, Wisconsin; 56. Scott Schwedes, WR, Syracuse; 99. Troy Stradford, WR, Boston College; 132. Chris Conlin, T, Penn State; 155. Lance Sellers, DB, Boise St.; 182. Tom Brown, RB, Pittsburgh; 210. Joel Williams, TE, Notre Dame; 212. Mark Dennis, T, Illinois; 237. Tim Pidgeon, LB, Syracuse; 266. Bobby Taylor, DB, Wisconsin; 293. Terence Mann, DT, SMU; 322. Jim Karsatos, QB, Ohio State.

Minnesota Vikings

14. D.J. Dozier, RB, Penn State; 44. Ray Berry, LB, Baylor; 72. Henry Thomas, DT, LSU; 100. Reginald Rutland, DB, Georgia Tech; 156. Greg Richardson, WR, Alabama; 211. Rick Fenney, RB, Washington; 239. Leonard Jones, DB, Texas Tech; 267. Bob Riley, T, Indiana; 295. Brent Pease, QB, Montana; 323. Keith Williams, DT, Florida

New England Patriots

23. Bruce Armstrong, G, Louisville; 79. Bob Perryman, RB, Michigan; 98. Richard Gannon, QB, Delaware; 102. Derrick Beasley, DB, Winston-Salem; 107. Tim Jordan, LB, Wisconsin; 113. Danny Villa, T, Arizona St.; 116. Tom Gibson, DE, Northern Arizona; 163. Gene Taylor, WR, Fresno St.; 302. Carlos Reveiz, K, Tennessee; 330. Elgin Davis, RB, Central Florida.

New Orleans Saints

11. Shawn Knight, DT, BYU; 40. Lonzell Hill, WR, Washington; 67. Michael Adams, DB, Arkansas St.; 96. Steve Trapilo, G, Boston College; 123. Milton Mack, DB, Alcorn St.; 152. Thomas Henley, WR, Stanford; 179. Gene Atkins, DB, Florida A&M; 207. Toi Cook, DB, Stanford; 234. Scott Leach, LB, Ohio St.; 263. Robert Clark, WR, No. Carolina Central; 290. Arthur Wells, TE, Grambling; 319. Tyrone Sorrells, T, Georgia Tech.

New York Giants

28. Mark Ingram, WR, Michigan St.; 55. Adrian White, DB, Florida; 84. Stephen Baker, WR, Fresno St.; 112. Odessa Turner, WR, NW Louisiana; 140. Paul O'Connor, G, Miami; 160. Tim Richardson, RB, Pacific; 168. Doug Riesenberg, T, California; 223. Rod Jones, TE, Washington; 225. Stan Parker, G, Nebraska; 251. Dana Wright, RB, Findlay; 279. Chuck Faucette, LB, Maryland; 307. Dave Walter, QB, Michigan Tech; 321. Bill Berthusen, DT, Iowa St.; 329. Chad Stark, RB, No. Dakota St.

New York Jets

21. Roger Vick, RB, Texas A&M; 42. Alex Gordon, LB, Cincinnati; 75. Onzy Elam, LB, Tennessee St.; 129. Kirby Jackson, DB, Mississippi St.; 161. Tracy Martin, WR, No. Dakota; 187. Gerald Nichols, DT, Florida St.; 196. Eddie Hunter, RB, Virginia Tech; 214. Mike Rice, WR, Montana; 247. Ron McLean, DE, Fullerton St.; 268. Sid Lewis, DB, Penn State; 300. Kirk Timmer, LB, Montana St.; 327. Bill Ransdell, QB, Kentucky.

Philadelphia Eagles

9. Jerome Brown, DT, Miami; 65. Ben Tamburello, C, Auburn; 93. Byron Evans, LB, Arizona; 121. David Alexander, G, Tulsa; 149. Ron Moten, LB, Florida; 158. Chris Pike, DT, Tulsa; 177, Brian Williams, T, Central Michigan; 232. Ken Lambiotte, QB, William & Mary; 260. Paul Carberry, DT, Oregon State; 316. Bobby Morse, RB, Michigan St.

Pittsburgh Steelers

10. Rod Woodson, DB, Purdue; 38. Delton Hall, DB, Clemson; 66. Charles Lockett, WR, Long Beach St.; 94. Thomas Everett, DB, Baylor; 122. Hardy Nickerson, LB, California; 141. Tim Johnson, DT, Penn State; 150. Greg Lloyd, LB, Fort Valley St.; 178. Chris Kelley, TE, Akron; 206. Charles Buchanan, DE, Tennessee St.; 233. Joey Clinkscales, WR, Tennessee; 261. Merrill Hoge, RB, Idaho St.; 289. Paul Oswald, C, Kansas; 317. Theo Young, TE, Arkansas

St. Louis Cardinals

6. Kelly Stouffer, QB, Colorado St.; 34. Tim McDonald, DB, Southern Cal; 62. Robert Awalt, TE, San Diego St.; 70. Colin Scotts, DT, Hawaii; 90. Rod Saddler, DT, Texas A&M; 118. George Swarn, RB, Miami (Ohio); 126. John Bruno, P, Penn State; 127. Ilia Jarostchuk, LB, New Hampshire; 146. Mark Garalczyk, DT, Western Michigan; 174. Tim Peoples, DB, Washington; 195. William Harris, TE, Bishop; 201. Steve Alvord, T, Washington; 229. Wayne Davis, LB, Alabama; 257. Charles Wright, DB, Tulsa; 285. Todd Peat, G, Northern Illinois.

San Diego Chargers

24. Rod Bernstine, TE, Texas A&M; 53. Louis Brock, DB, Southern Cal; 59. Karl Wilson, DE, LSU; 89. Mark Vlasic, QB, Iowa; 115. Nelson Jones, DB, No. Carolina St.; 173. Jamie Holland, WR, Ohio State; 199. Joe MacEsker, T, Texas-El Paso; 204. Ron Brown, LB, Southern Cal; 226. Thomas Wilcher, RB, Michigan; 256. Anthony Anderson, DB, Grambling; 283. Joe Goebel, C, UCLA; 310. Marcus Greenwood, RB, UCLA.

San Francisco 49ers

22. Harris Barton, T, No. Carolina; 25. Terrence Flagler, RB, Clemson; 37. Jeff Bregel, G, Southern Cal; 134. Paul Jokisch, WR, Michigan; 162. Bob White, LB, Penn State; 189. Steve DeLine, K, Colorado St.; 217. David Grayson, LB, Fresno St.; 245. Jonathan Shelley, DB, Mississippi; 274. John Paye, QB, Stanford; 301. Calvin Nicholas, WR, Grambling.

Seattle Seahawks

18. Tony Woods, DE, Pittsburgh; 45. David Wyman, LB, Stanford; 104. Mark Moore, DB, Oklahoma St.; 119. Tommie Agee, RB, Auburn; 131. Ruben Rodriguez, P, Arizona; 184. Roland Barbay, T, LSU; 185. Derek Tennell, TE, UCLA; 216. Sammy Garza, QB, Texas-El Paso; 243. M.L. Johnson, LB, Hawaii; 270. Louis Clark, TE, Mississippi St.; 297. Darryl Oliver, RB, Miami; 312. Wes Dove, DE, Syracuse; 324. Tony Burse, RB, Middle Tennessee St.

Tampa Bay Buccaneers

1. Vinny Testaverde, QB, Miami; 36. Ricky Reynolds, DB, Washington St.; 50. Winston Moss, LB, Miami; 51. Don Smith, RB, Mississippi St.; 57. Mark Carrier, WR, Nicholls St.; 85. Don Graham, LB, Penn State; 87. Ron Hall, TE, Hawaii; 106. Bruce Hill, WR, Arizona St.; 135. Henry Rolling, LB, Nevada-Reno; 137. Tony Mayes, DB, Kentucky; 143. Steve Bartalo, RB, Colorado St.; 169. Curt Jarvis, DT, Alabama; 190. Harry Swayne, DT, Rutgers; 197. Stan Mataele, DT, Arizona; 224. Joe Armentrout, RB, Wisconsin; 246. Greg Davis, P, The Citadel; 252. Mike Simmonds, G, Indiana St.; 280. Reggie Taylor, RB, Cincinnati; 308. Scott Cooper, DT, Kearney St.; 313. Mike Shula, QB, Alabama.

Washington Redskins

30. Brian Davis, DB, Nebraska; 48. Wally Kleine, T, Notre Dame; 117. Tim Smith, RB, Texas Tech; 144. Steve Gage, DB, Tulsa; 164. Ed Simmons, T, Eastern Washington; 192. Johnny Thomas, DB, Baylor; 219. Clarence Vaughn, LB, Northern Illinois; 248. Alfred Jenkins, RB, Arizona; 275. Ted Wilson, WR, Central Florida; 304. Laron Brown, WR, Texas; 331. Ray Hitchcock, C, Minnesota.

1986 Statistics

Leading Rushers	Att.	Yards	Avg.	Long	TDs
AFC					
Warner, Sea.	319	1481	4.6	60	13
Brooks, Cin.	205	1087	5.3	56	5
Jackson, Pitt.	216	910	4.2	31	5
Abercrombie, Pitt.	214	877	4.1	38	6
McNeil, Jets	214	856	4.0	40	5
Hampton, Mia.	186	830	4.5	54	9
Winder, Den.	240	789	3.3	31	9
Allen, Raiders	208	759	3.6	28	5
Mack, Cle.	174	665	3.8	20	10
Rozier, Hou.	199	662	3.3	19	4
Riddick, Buff.	150	632	4.2	41	4
McMillan, Ind.	189	609	3.2	28	3
Hector, Jets.	164	605	3.7	41	8
Williams, Sea.	129	538	4.2	36	0
McCallum, Raiders	142	536	3.8	18	1
Dickey, Cle.	135	523	3.9	47	6
Kinnebrew, Cin.	131	519	4.0	39	8
Pruitt, K.C.	139	448	3.2	16	2
Anderson, S.D.	127	442	3.5	17	1
James, N.E.	154	427	2.8	16	4
NFC					
Dickerson, Rams	404	1821	4.5	42	11
Morris, Giants	341	1516	4.4	54	14

Leading Rushers	Att.	Yards	Avg.	Long	TDs
Mayes, N.O.	286	1353	4.7	50	8
Payton, Chi.	321	1333	4.2	41	8
Riggs, Atl.	343	1327	3.9	31	9
Rogers, Wash.	303	1203	4.0	42	18
Jones, Det.	252	903	3.6	39	8
Craig, S.F.	204	830	4.1	25	7
Mitchell, St. L.	174	800	4.6	44	5
Nelson, Minn.	191	793	4.2	42	4
Dorsett, Dall.	184	748	4.1	33	5
Walker, Dall.	151	737	4.9	84	12
Wilder, T.B.	190	704	3.7	45	2
James, Det.	159	688	4.3	60	3
Cribbs, S.F.	152	590	3.9	19	5
Byars, Phil.	177	577	3.3	32	1
Ferrell, St. L.	124	548	4.4	25	0
Cunningham, Phil.	66	540	8.2	20	5
Davis, G.B.	114	519	4.6	50	0
Redden, Rams	110	467	4.2	41	4

Leading Passers	Att.	Comp.	Yds. Gnd.	TD Pass	Int.	Rating
AFC						
Marino, Mia.	623	378	4746	44	23	95.2
Krieg, Sea.	375	225	2921	21	11	91.0
Eason, N.E.	448	276	3328	19	10	89.2
Esiason, Cin.	469	273	3959	24	17	87.7
O'Brien, Jets	482	300	3690	25	20	85.8
Kosar, Cle.	531	310	3854	17	10	83.8
Kelly, Buff.	480	285	3593	22	17	83.3
Plunkett, Raiders	252	133	1986	14	9	82.5
Elway, Den.	504	280	3485	19	13	79.0
Fouts, S.D.	430	252	3031	16	22	71.4
Kenney, K.C.	308	161	1922	13	11	70.8
Wilson, Raiders	240	129	1721	12	15	67.4
Malone, Pitt.	425	216	2444	15	18	62.5
Moon, Hou.	488	256	3489	13	26	62.3

Leading Passers	Att.	Comp.	Yds. Gnd	TD Pass	Int.	Rat- ing
NFC						
Kramer, Minn.	372	208	3000	24	10	92.6
Montana, S.F.	307	191	2236	8	9	80.7
Hipple, Det.	305	192	1919	9	11	75.6
Simms, Giants	468	259	3487	21	22	74.6
Lomax, St. L.	421	240	2583	13	12	73.6
Schroeder, Wash.	541	276	4109	22	22	72.9
Archer, Atl.	294	150	2007	10	9	71.6
Jaworski, Phil.	245	128	1405	8	6	70.2
Pelluer, Dall.	378	215	2727	8	17	67.9
Wright, G.B.	492	263	3247	17	23	66.2
Wilson, N.O.	342	189	2353	10	17	65.8
Young, T.B.	363	195	2282	8	13	65.5

Leading Receivers	No.	Yards	Avg.	TDs
AFC				
Christensen, Raiders	95	1153	12.1	8
Toon, Jets	85	1176	13.8	8
Morgan, N.E.	84	1491	17.8	10
Anderson, S.D.	80	871	10.9	8
Collins, N.E.	77	684	8.9	5
Bouza, Ind.	71	830	11.7	5
Largent, Sea.	70	1070	15.3	9
Shuler, Jets	69	675	9.8	4
Duper, Mia.	67	1313	19.6	11
Brooks, Ind.	65	1131	17.4	8
Hill, Hou.	65	1112	17.1	5
Winslow, S.D.	64	728	11.4	5
Willhite, Den.	64	529	8.3	3
Collinsworth, Cin.	62	1024	16.5	10
Givins, Hou.	61	1062	17.4	3
Hampton, Mia.	61	446	7.3	3
Clayton, Mia.	60	1150	19.2	10
Brown, Cin.	58	964	16.6	4
Chandler, S.D.	56	874	15.6	4

Leading Receivers	No.	Yards	Avg.	TDs
NFC				
Rice, S.F.	86	1570	18.3	15
Craig, S.F.	81	624	7.7	0
Smith, St. L.	80	1014	12.7	6
Walker, Dall.	76	837	11.0	2
Clark, Wash.	74	1265	17.1	7
Monk, Wash.	73	1068	14.6	4
Bavaro, Giants	66	1001	15.2	4
Lofton, G.B.	64	840	13.1	4
Brown, Atl.	63	918	14.6	4
Clark, S.F.	61	794	13.0	2
Quick, Phil.	60	939	15.7	9
Jordan, Minn.	58	859	14.8	6
Ferrell, St. L.	56	434	7.8	3
Jones, Det.	54	334	6.2	1
Chadwick, Det.	53	995	18.8	5

Leading Interceptors	No.	Yards	Long	TDs
AFC				
Cherry, K.C.	9	150	49	0
Lippett, N.E.	8	76	43	0
McElroy, Raiders	7	105	28	0
Breeden, Cin.	7	72	36	1
Harden, Den.	6	179	52	2
Holmes, Jets	6	29	28	0
Burruss, K.C.	5	193	72	3
Brown, Sea.	5	58	24	1
NFC				
Lott, S.F.	10	134	57	1
Waymer, N.O.	9	48	17	0
Lee, G.B.	9	33	11	0
Gray, Rams	8	101	28	0
Holt, Minn.	8	54	27	0
Richardson, Chi.	7	69	32	0
Irvin, Rams	6	150	50	1
Duerson, Chi.	6	139	38	0

Leading Scorers, Kicking	PAT	FG	Long	TP
AFC				
Franklin, N.E.	44/45	32/41	49	140
Johnson, Sea.	42/42	22/35	54	108
Karlis, Den.	44/45	20/28	51	104
Breech, Cin.	50/51	17/32	51	101
Lowery, K.C.	43/43	19/26	47	100
Bahr, Raiders	36/36	21/28	52	99
Anderson, Pitt.	32/32	21/32	45	95
Reveiz, Mia.	52/55	14/22	52	94
Zendejas, Hou.	28/29	22/27	51	94
Leahy, Jets	44/44	16/19	50	92
NFC				
Butler, Chi.	36/37	28/41	52	120
Wersching, S.F.	41/42	25/35	50	116
Nelson, Minn.	44/47	22/28	53	110
Andersen, N.O.	30/30	26/30	53	108
Allegre, Giants	33/33	24/32	46	105
Septien, Dall.	43/43	15/21	50	88
McFadden, Phil.	26/27	20/31	50	86
Lansford, Rams	34/35	17/24	50	85
Murray, Det.	31/32	18/25	52	85
Del Greco, G.B.	29/29	17/27	50	80

Leading Scorers, Touchdowns	TDs	Rush	Rec.	Ret.	TP
AFC					
Winder, Den.	14	9	5	0	84
Warner, Sea.	13	13	0	0	78
Hampton, Mia.	12	9	3	0	72
Walker, Jets	12	0	12	0	72
Duper, Mia.	11	0	11	0	66
Paige, K.C.	11	0	11	0	66
Clayton, Mia.	10	0	10	0	60
Collinsworth, Cin.	10	0	10	0	60
Mack, Cle.	10	10	0	0	60
Morgan, N.E.	10	0	10	0	60

Leading Scorers, Touchdowns	TDs	Rush	Rec.	Ret.	TP
NFC					
Rogers, Wash.	18	18	0	0	108
Rice, S.F.	16	1	15	0	96
Morris, Giants	15	14	1	0	90
Walker, Dall.	14	12	2	0	84
Dickerson, Rams	11	11	0	0	66
Payton, Chi.	11	8	3	0	66
Jones, Det.	9	8	1	0	54
Quick, Phil.	9	0	9	0	54
Riggs, Atl.	9	9	0	0	54
Mayes, N.O.	8	8	0	0	48

Leading Punters	No.	Yards	Long	Avg.
AFC				
Stark, Ind.	76	3432	63	45.2
Roby, Mia.	56	2476	73	44.2
Camarillo, N.E.	89	3746	64	42.1
Mojsiejenko, S.D.	72	3026	62	42.0
Gossett, Cle.	83	3423	61	41.2
Johnson, Hou.	88	3623	66	41.2
Colbert, K.C.	99	4033	56	40.7
Kidd, Buff.	75	3031	57	40.4
Guy, Raiders	90	3620	64	40.2
Newsome, Pitt.	86	3447	64	40.1
Jennings, Jets	85	3353	55	39.4
Gamache, Sea.	79	3048	55	38.6
Hayes, Cin.	56	1965	52	35.1
NFC				
Landeta, Giants	79	3539	61	44.8
Donnelly, Atl.	78	3421	71	43.9
Cox, Wash.	75	3271	58	43.6
Hansen, N.O.	81	3456	66	42.7
Teltschik, Phil.	108	4493	62	41.6

Leading Punters	No.	Yards	Long	Avg.
Runager, S.F.	83	3450	62	41.6
Coleman, Minn.	67	2774	69	41.4
Buford, Chi.	69	2850	59	41.3
Saxon, Dall.	86	3498	58	40.7
Garcia, T.B.	77	3089	60	40.1
Bracken, G.B.	55	2203	63	40.1
Black, Det.	46	1819	57	39.5
Hatcher, Rams	97	3740	57	38.6
Cater, St. L.	61	2271	52	37.2

Leading Punt Returners	No.	Yards	Avg.	TDs
AFC				
Edmonds, Sea.	34	419	12.3	1
Willhite, Den.	42	468	11.1	1
Fryar, N.E.	35	366	10.5	1
Anderson, S.D.	25	227	9.1	0
Walker, Raiders	49	440	9.0	1
Woods, Pitt.	33	294	8.9	0
McNeil, Cle.	40	348	8.7	1
Smith, K.C.	29	245	8.4	0
Sohn, Jets	35	289	8.3	0
Drewrey, Hou	34	262	7.7	0
NFC				
Sikahema, Sea.	43	522	12.1	2
Griffin, S.F.	38	377	9.9	1
Mandley, Det.	43	420	9.8	1
Jenkins, Wash.	28	270	9.6	0
Stanley, G.B.	33	316	9.6	1
Martin, N.O.	24	227	9.5	0
Barnes, Chi.	57	482	8.5	0
Sutton, Rams	28	234	8.4	0
McConkey, Giants	32	253	7.9	0
Bess, Minn.	23	162	7.0	0

Leading Kickoff Returners	No.	Yards	Avg.	TDs
AFC				
Sanchez, Pitt.	25	591	23.6	0
McGee, Cin.	43	1007	23.4	0
Humphery, Jets	28	655	23.4	1
Bell, Den.	23	531	23.1	0
Lang, Den.	21	480	22.9	0
Edmonds, Sea.	34	764	22.5	0
Starring, N.E.	36	802	22.3	0
Ellis, Mia.	25	541	21.6	0
Bentley, Ind.	32	687	21.5	0
Adams, Raiders	27	573	21.2	2
NFC				
Gentry, Chi.	20	576	28.8	1
Gray, N.O.	31	866	27.9	1
Sikahema, St. L.	37	847	22.9	0
Bess, Minn.	31	705	22.7	0
Brown, Rams	36	794	22.1	0
Stamps, Atl.	24	514	21.4	0
Hunter, Det.	49	1007	20.6	0
Jenkins, Wash.	27	554	20.5	0
Stanley, G.B.	28	559	20.0	0
Elder, Pitt.	22	435	19.8	0

1987
NFL Schedule

Sunday, September 13
N.Y. Jets at Buffalo
Cincinnati at Indianap.
Cleveland at New Orleans
Seattle at Denver
L.A. Rams at Houston
San Diego at Kansas City
L.A. Raiders at Green Bay
Miami at New England
San Fran. at Pittsburgh
Atlanta at Tampa Bay
Dallas at St. Louis
Detroit at Minnesota
Philadelphia at Wash.

Monday, September 14
N.Y. Giants at Chicago

Sunday, September 20
Houston at Buffalo
San Fran. at Cincinnati
Pittsburgh at Cleveland
Denver vs. Green Bay
  at Milwaukee
Miami at Indianapolis
Kansas City at Seattle
Detroit at L.A. Raiders
St. Louis at San Diego
Washington at Atlanta
Tampa Bay at Chicago
Dallas at N.Y. Giants
Minnesota at L.A. Rams
New Orleans at Phil.

Monday, September 21
New England at N.Y. Jets

Sunday, September 27
Buffalo at Dallas
Cincinnati at L.A. Rams
L.A. Raiders at Houston
Indianapolis at St. Louis
Minnesota at Kansas City
N.Y. Giants at Miami
New England at Wash.
N.Y. Jets at Pittsburgh
Seattle at San Diego
Atlanta at New Orleans
Chicago at Detroit
Green Bay at Tampa Bay
Philadelphia at San Fran.

Monday, September 28
Denver at Cleveland

Sunday, October 4
Indianapolis at Buffalo
San Diego at Cincinnati
Cleveland at New England
Houston at Denver
Kan. City at L.A. Raiders
Miami at Seattle
Dallas at N.Y. Jets
Pittsburgh at Atlanta
Chicago at Philadelphia
Tampa Bay at Detroit
Green Bay at Minnesota

L.A. Rams at New Orleans
St. Louis at Washington

Monday, October 5
San Fran. at N.Y. Giants

Sunday, October 11
Buffalo at New England
Cincinnati at Seattle
Houston at Cleveland
N.Y. Jets at Indianapolis
Kansas City at Miami
Pittsburgh at L.A. Rams
San Diego at Tampa Bay
Washington at N.Y. Giants
Atlanta at San Fran.
Minnesota at Chicago
Philadelphia at Dallas
Detroit at Green Bay
New Orleans at St. Louis

Monday, October 12
L.A. Raiders at Denver

Sunday, October 18
N.Y. Giants at Buffalo
Cleveland at Cincinnati
Denver at Kansas City
New England at Houston
Indianapolis at Pittsburgh
San Diego at L.A. Raiders
Miami at N.Y. Jets
Seattle at Detroit
L.A. Rams at Atlanta
New Orleans at Chicago
Philadelphia at Green Bay
Tampa Bay at Minnesota
St. Louis at San Fran.

Monday, October 19
Washington at Dallas

Sunday, October 25
Buffalo at Miami
Cincinnati at Pittsburgh
Denver at Minnesota
Atlanta at Houston
New England at Indianap.
Seattle at L.A. Raiders
N.Y. Jets at Washington
Kansas City at San Diego
Chicago at Tampa Bay
Dallas at Philadelphia
Green Bay at Detroit
San Fran. at New Orleans
St. Louis at N.Y. Giants

Monday, October 26
L.A. Rams at Cleveland

Sunday, November 1
Washington at Buffalo
Houston at Cincinnati
Cleveland at San Diego
Detroit at Denver
Indianapolis at N.Y. Jets
Kansas City at Chicago
L.A. Raiders at New Eng.
Pittsburgh at Miami
Minnesota at Seattle
New Orleans at Atlanta
Tampa Bay vs. Green Bay
    at Milwaukee
San Fran. at L.A. Rams
Philadelphia at St. Louis

Monday, Nov. 2
N.Y. Giants at Dallas

Sunday, November 8
Denver at Buffalo
Miami at Cincinnati
Houston at San Fran.
San Diego at Indianapolis

Pittsburgh at Kansas City
L.A. Raiders at Minnesota
New Eng. at N.Y. Giants
Atlanta at Cleveland
Chicago at Green Bay
Dallas at Detroit
New Orleans at L.A. Rams
Washington at Phil.
Tampa Bay at St. Louis

Monday, November 9
Seattle at N.Y. Jets

Sunday, November 15
Buffalo at Cleveland
Cincinnati at Atlanta
Houston at Pittsburgh
Indianapolis at Miami
N.Y. Jets at Kansas City
L.A. Raiders at San Diego
Dallas at New England
Green Bay at Seattle
Detroit at Washington
L.A. Rams at St. Louis
Minnesota at Tampa Bay
New Orleans at San Fran.
N.Y. Giants at Phil.

Monday, November 16
Chicago at Denver

Sunday, November 22
Buffalo at N.Y. Jets
Pittsburgh at Cincinnati
Cleveland at Houston
Denver at L.A. Raiders
Indianap. at New England
Green Bay at Kansas City
Miami at Dallas
San Diego at Seattle
Atlanta at Minnesota
Detroit at Chicago

N.Y. Giants at New Orleans
St. Louis at Philadelphia
San Fran. at Tampa Bay

Monday, November 23
L.A. Rams at Washington

Thursday, November 26
Kansas City at Detroit
Minnesota at Dallas

Sunday, November 29
Miami at Buffalo
Cincinnati at N.Y. Jets
Cleveland at San Fran.
Denver at San Diego
Houston at Indianapolis
Philadelphia at New England
New Orleans at Pittsburgh
St. Louis at Atlanta
Green Bay at Chicago
Tampa Bay at L.A. Rams
N.Y. Giants at Washington

Monday, November 30
L.A. Raiders at Seattle

Sunday, December 6
Buffalo at L.A. Raiders
Kansas City at Cincinnati
Indianapolis at Cleveland
New England at Denver
San Diego at Houston
Seattle at Pittsburgh
Atlanta at Dallas
Chicago at Minnesota
San Fran. at Green Bay
L.A. Rams at Detroit
Tampa Bay at New Orleans
Phil. at N.Y. Giants
Washington at St. Louis

Monday, December 7
N.Y. Jets at Miami

Sunday, December 13
Buffalo at Indianapolis
Cincinnati at Cleveland
Denver at Seattle
Houston at New Orleans
L.A. Raiders at Kan. City
Miami at Philadelphia
N.Y. Jets at New England
Pittsburgh at San Diego
Atlanta at L.A. Rams
Dallas at Washington
Detroit at Tampa Bay
Minnesota vs. Green Bay
  at Milwaukee
N.Y. Giants at St. Louis

Monday, December 14
Chicago at San Fran.

Saturday, December 19
Green Bay at N.Y. Giants
Kansas City at Denver

Sunday, December 20
New England at Buffalo
New Orleans at Cincinnati
Cleveland at L.A. Raiders
Pittsburgh at Houston

Indianapolis at San Diego
Washington at Miami
Philadelphia at N.Y. Jets
Seattle at Chicago
San Fran. at Atlanta
Minnesota at Detroit
St. Louis at Tampa Bay

Monday, December 21
Dallas at L.A. Rams

Saturday, December 26
Cleveland at Pittsburgh
Washington at Minnesota

Sunday, December 27
Buffalo at Philadelphia
Cincinnati at Houston
San Diego at Denver
Tampa Bay at Indianapolis
Seattle at Kansas City
Chicago at L.A. Raiders
N.Y. Jets at N.Y. Giants
Detroit at Atlanta
St. Louis at Dallas
Green Bay at New Orleans
L.A. Rams at San Fran.

Monday, December 28
New England at Miami

BRUCE WEBER PICKS
HOW THEY'LL FINISH IN 1987

AFC East
1. Miami
2. New England
3. N.Y. Jets
4. Buffalo
5. Indianapolis

AFC Central
1. Cleveland
2. Pittsburgh
3. Cincinnati
4. Houston

AFC West
1. Seattle
2. L.A. Raiders
3. Denver
4. Kansas City
5. San Diego

NFC East
1. Washington
2. N.Y. Giants
3. Dallas
4. Philadelphia
5. St. Louis

NFC Central
1. Chicago
2. Minnesota
3. Green Bay
4. Detroit
5. Tampa Bay

NFC West
1. L.A. Rams
2. New Orleans
3. San Francisco
4. Atlanta

Wild Cards: New England, L.A. Raiders, N.Y. Giants, Minnesota

AFC Champions: Cleveland
NFC Champions: L.A. Rams
Super Bowl Champions: L.A. Rams

YOU PICK
HOW THEY'LL FINISH IN 1987

AFC East

1.
2.
3.
4.
5.

AFC Central

1. Cleveland
2. Pittsburg
3. Houston
4. Cincinnati

AFC West

1.
2.
3.
4.
5.

NFC East

1.
2.
3.
4.
5.

NFC Central

1.
2.
3.
4.
5.

NFC West

1.
2.
3.
4.

Wild Cards:

AFC Champions:

NFC Champions:

Super Bowl Champions: